TOWARD AN ATLANTIC COMMUNITY

TOWARD AN ATLANTIC COMMUNITY

by CHRISTIAN A. HERTER

Published for the
Council on Foreign Relations
by
Harper & Row, Publishers
New York and Evanston

For a list of Council publications see pages *106* and *107*.

IN MEMORY OF EDWARD JOHN NOBLE

The Policy Book series of the Council on Foreign Relations is published under a grant from the Edward John Noble Foundation in memory of Mr. Noble and his interest in encouraging American leadership in international affairs.

Policy Books of the Council on Foreign Relations

This volume is the fourth in the Council on Foreign Relations' new series of short books on important issues of United States foreign policy. Their purpose is twofold: first, to provide readers in this country and elsewhere with essays and analytical studies of the highest quality on problems of world significance; and, second, to contribute to constructive thinking on American policies for the future. These volumes make a virtue of brevity, not with the aim of oversimplification, but to present with a minimum of factual background and detail the reasoned conclusions of individual authors with first-hand experience and special qualifications.

The Council was fortunate in persuading a former Secretary of State, Mr. Christian A. Herter, to write this book on the Atlantic Community. His distinguished public career, which also included service as Member of Congress, Governor of Massachusetts, and Under Secretary of State, lends great weight to his views.

While the book was in preparation, Mr. Herter had the benefit of the advice and comments of a small group invited to discuss his manuscript. The Council wishes to thank the following, who were present at that meeting: Hamilton Fish Armstrong, W. Randolph Burgess, John C. Campbell, James B. Conant, George S. Franklin, Jr.,

Gardner Patterson, Arnold Wolfers, and Henry M. Wriston. Philip E. Mosely, Principal Research Fellow at the Council, and John C. Campbell, who is in charge of the series of Policy Books, consulted with the author from time to time on both substance and editorial aspects of the book.

Responsibility for the statements of fact and opinion rests with the author, not with the group or the Council. The Council takes responsibility for the decision to publish the book as a contribution to thought on a subject of the greatest moment: present and future relationships among the nations of the Atlantic world.

Contents

TOWARD AN ATLANTIC COMMUNITY

A Call to Action

We, the citizen delegates to the Atlantic Convention of NATO Nations, meeting in Paris, January 8–20, 1962, are convinced that our survival as free men, and the possibility of progress for all men, demand the creation of a true Atlantic Community within the next decade, . . .

With these words nearly one hundred citizens from fourteen NATO nations introduced a statement of the urgent challenge to action that faces the nations of the free world. Issued on January 19, 1962, the Declaration of Paris emphasizes three separate but interrelated elements of policy—survival, progress, community. Each of them deserves separate consideration. But before examining them it may be helpful to say a few words on who were the citizen authors of the Declaration, and how they came to assemble in Paris.

In September 1960 the Congress of the United States passed a law creating a Citizens Committee of twenty members, to be appointed by the Speaker of the House and the President of the Senate, whose responsibility it was to meet, if possible, with similar groups from the other NATO countries in order to explore ways in which the NATO alliance and the Atlantic Community could be strengthened, particularly in political and economic fields. Appointments to the Citizens Committee were not made until March 1961, and the group so appointed then organized and approached legislative leaders in the other NATO countries with the view to having similar committees appointed.

A preliminary group met in London in the fall of 1961, and a convention was organized to meet in Paris early in 1962. It was my privilege to serve as a member of the American citizens group; and Mr. Will Clayton of Houston, Texas, and I were elected co-chairmen of this group. The convention held in Paris was made up of individuals who could speak only for themselves without any authority from their governments, although many of the individuals were active members of legislative bodies of their respective nations.

The three separate thoughts developed in the statement quoted above concern first, the stark challenge to the survival of free men; second, the possibility of progress for all men; and third, the necessity for the creation of a true Atlantic Community within the next decade. It is the purpose of this short book to examine each of these separate but related matters and to conclude with recommendations which, without promising any final solutions to the problems raised, might well stimulate action which governments alone can take in order to achieve a "true Atlantic Community."

Chapter I

"Our Survival as Free Men"

Since World War II revolutionary changes have taken place. Probably the most important and certainly the most dangerous of these has been the combination of the rapid growth in the power of the Soviet Union, the formation of the bloc of Communist nations, and the declared intention of the leaders of that bloc to bring the whole of the world under Communist domination.

Every action taken by the Soviet leaders since 1947 confirms in my mind the genuineness of the Communist conviction that their goal is attainable. In other words, I take their statements at face value and, hence, am convinced that the survival of free men is being seriously threatened, and that it is incumbent upon the free nations of the world to take such steps as will minimize the threat or reduce it to the vanishing point.

In 1947 Secretary of State Marshall took the initiative in suggesting a new program of American aid to Europe if the European nations themselves could work out national plans for their own recovery. Foreign Ministers Ernest Bevin of the United Kingdom and Georges Bidault of France, after a preliminary meeting with Soviet Foreign Minister Molotov at which Russia's refusal to cooperate was made quite clear, invited twenty-two European nations to a conference in Paris. The purpose of the meeting was to discuss what steps could be taken by those nations, in conjunction with the assistance which the United States might be able to render, in order to restore as rapidly as possible the war-torn economy of Europe. States which had been neutral in the recent war, as well as the "satellite" nations of Eastern Europe, were among those invited. The U.S.S.R., not content with its own abstention, went even farther. It brought pressure to bear upon Poland, Czechoslovakia and the other nations of Eastern Europe to stay away also. This was the clearest indication yet given that Soviet Russia preferred the deepening division of Europe to a genuine effort to rebuild it, that she would no longer cooperate with Western Europe and the United States and Canada, her previous partners, and would go it alone.

Soon thereafter the government of Czechoslovakia was captured by the Communists. By that time other nations of Eastern Europe had become satellites in the Soviet bloc. And nations outside that bloc were being threatened by Soviet pressure from without or by armed Communist violence from within. But only after the blockade of Berlin by the Soviet Union in 1948 did the Western nations react with the serious step of formally joining together for their own protection. The North Atlantic Treaty Organization (NATO) was formed, an alliance first of twelve nations and later expanded by the addition of Greece and Turkey and then the Federal Republic of Germany.[1]

Soon after Germany had been brought into NATO in 1955, the Russians countered by organizing their satellite countries into a military alliance with the U.S.S.R., the Warsaw Pact,[2] although this was in effect only a gesture

[1] The original members were Belgium, Canada, Denmark, France, Great Britain, Holland, Iceland, Italy, Luxembourg, Norway, Portugal and the United States.

[2] The Warsaw Pact included the U.S.S.R., Poland, East Germany, Czechoslovakia, Hungary, Bulgaria, Rumania and Albania. Albania has

since Russia's military dominance and even military occupation of the countries of that alliance had already created a monolithic bloc in Eastern Europe.

NATO was created for defensive purposes. It conforms to the Charter of the United Nations, previously signed by most NATO members and adhered to by others upon Admission to the United Nations. Articles 51 and 52 of the Charter specifically recognize the right of collective self-defense and permit the creation of regional defense groupings of nations.

NATO is only one of a series of defensive regional alliances. The Treaty of Rio de Janeiro of 1947 created a similar alliance in the Western Hemisphere, consisting of all the nations of Latin America plus the United States, in which each nation pledged itself to defend the others in the event of aggressive action against any one of them. Later the pattern of alliances and regional security organizations was extended to the Far East and the Middle East. In 1951 a security arrangement known as ANZUS was signed by the United States, Australia and New Zealand. Three years later, after the Communist success in Indo-China, the SEATO alliance was formed, consisting of the United States, Great Britain, France, Australia, New Zealand, the Philippines, Thailand and Pakistan. Soon thereafter, with the United States taking a large part of the initiative, the Baghdad Pact was signed. This treaty provided for a defensive alliance of Pakistan, Iran, Iraq, Turkey and Great Britain. The United States itself did not formally join but has participated in the work of all the committees of that alliance. After the revolution in Iraq in 1958, the Iraqi government withdrew from the alliance and the defensive group then changed its name to CENTO.

By way of completing what was in effect a "containment policy"—a policy which aimed at binding together in de-

now ceased to be an active member of the alliance, although no public announcement of its withdrawal or expulsion has been made.

fensive arrangements many of the nations peripheral to the Communist bloc—the United States had concluded separate defensive treaties with Japan in 1951 (which was replaced by the later treaty of 1960), with the Republic of Korea, and with the Nationalist Chinese government in Taiwan.

My reason for listing these various treaties is to give emphasis to the genuine fear in most of the free nations of active military aggression on the part of the Communist powers threatening the survival of the citizens of those nations as free men. The treaties are not just the product of an American concern about Communist expansion and the world balance of power. They reflect also the concerns of the nations which are our partners, their search for security, and their will to defend their own independence.

In the last eight years the Communist bloc has not increased by force of arms the physical territory over which it has control, though it retained control of Hungary in 1956 by military action. While Cuba today must be considered a part of this bloc, it was taken over by internal subversion and infiltration, and not by external military aggression.

The possibility of military aggression, however, is still a very real and present danger. It has caused the continuing arms build-up in the Western world, stimulated first by the Korean war and then by the development of the increasingly strong nuclear capability in Russia. The Western arms effort does not take place in a vacuum. It reflects directly the growth of Soviet armed strength, the Soviet refusal to agree on arms control and disarmament, and the continuing Communist pressure on the free world despite talk of peaceful coexistence.

There may be differences of view as to the likelihood of the Soviet Union's unleashing nuclear war, but there is no difference of view among free-world leaders with regard to the intentions of the Communist powers to bring into the Communist camp as many nations as possible through subversion and revolution and economic warfare. It is important, therefore, to take a realistic look at the geographic and economic composition of the nations of the world. The Communist bloc—and it must still be considered a bloc despite current Soviet-Chinese differences—comprises roughly one-third of the people of the world, situated, with the exception of Albania and Cuba, in a single continuous land mass. Their standard of living, in spite of the advances made in the Soviet system and the inclusion in the bloc of relatively advanced states such as Czechoslovakia and East Germany, is on the whole low. The highly developed industrial nations of the world, located, with the exception of Japan, in Western Europe and the Atlantic area, have only about one-sixth of the world's population and occupy one-sixth of the earth's surface. Their standard of living is far higher.

The balance, or more than one-half, of the world's peoples live in nations or dependencies in what are termed the less developed areas of the world. They have, for the most part, a very low living standard. The average annual income of the people of these nations is less than one-fifteenth of that in the United States. Among the less developed nations, some of which are self-proclaimed neutrals while others are allied or associated with the West, there are over fifty which have gained independence since the Charter of the United Nations was signed, a revolutionary change in world politics. Roughly thirty of them have become independent in the last four years.

While there is no indication that the Communist powers are necessarily contemplating open and direct military action against any of these nations, a process of subversion through all the wiles that have become commonplace in Soviet tactics is, nevertheless, actively under way in order to bring these nations into the Communist camp. Guerrilla warfare such as we are witnessing in Laos and Viet-Nam is part of the process. Certainly Communist China's repeated assertion that she will conquer Taiwan by force is another reality. The revolution in Cuba, camouflaged in its early stages by solemn declarations of anticommunism and loyalty to democratic principles, now stands revealed as Communist-inspired and Communist-led, serving the interests of the Soviet Union and not those of Cuba. The conditions of poverty and misery existing in so many of these less developed nations were not created by the Communists; however, accompanied as they are today by the so-called "revolution of rising expectations," they may serve the Communist cause well in that they create widespread dissatisfaction and a fertile field for Communist infiltration and propaganda. This threat to the freedom and independence of new nations having so brief an experience with them is extraordinarily difficult to combat.

This is a sketchy outline of the depressing reality of our world. But there is more than this in the threat to the survival of free men. The Communists also seek to create disunity among the highly industrialized nations of the free world. In a number of these nations there exist strong Communist or pro-Communist minorities, often including substantial numbers of public officials either in the legislatures or the municipal governments. Directed by Moscow or by Peking, these Communist minorities exercise a powerful influence to cause not only internal political dissensions, but also divisions between the free nations. So does Soviet diplomacy. In other words, the Communist strategy for the conquest of the world lies in two principal directions: first, to take or win over the less developed nations; and second, to intimidate, disrupt, and divide the great industrial nations, so as to weaken them from a military, economic, political, and psychological point of view and thus to speed the inevitable triumph of communism.

The second consideration raised in the quotation from the Declaration of Paris is that of "the possibility of progress for all men." The implication of this consideration obviously reflects a deep concern to improve the status of human beings in large sections of the world. I earlier mentioned some cold figures. They tell part of the story but not all. Nature, geography and history have treated nations very unequally. Some have raw materials, development of which can provide exports which permit economic gains. Others do not. In some nations, there is good soil and a favorable climate for agricultural development. In others, there are climatic conditions which sap the energies of human beings. Some have the basic physical and human requirements for industrialization. Others have neither the resources nor the skills.

Because of variations in conditions, in addition to those of size and population, it is impossible to apply the same yardsticks in describing the reasons for the economic woes of less developed countries. One can, however, identify a few common denominators applicable in areas where living standards are low. Illiteracy and disease are the most prominent. The skills needed to take advantage of known production techniques are generally lacking. Until recently, communications between the more highly developed countries and the peoples of the less developed countries were most limited; and colonial repressions have played their part. In these fields some progress is now being made; but that progress has brought with it both physical and psychological complications. Opening up of communications and the increasing literacy of the people have brought an awareness of their backwardness and poverty without clear assurance that their lot is improvable. Extraordinary progress in health measures, while admirable, is tending to increase the size of the population, not so much because of an increased birth rate but because of the longer life span of the individual. When unaccompanied by corresponding economic growth, this rapid rise in sheer numbers of people has inevitably frustrated hopes for an increasing standard of living.

The United States has invested many tens of billions in aid in an effort to give these impoverished, awakening peoples the hope of seeing a better life ahead. The Communists have made much smaller economic efforts, but have coupled those efforts everywhere with attempts to create political situations favorable to the spread of communism. It is only too obvious that if there is to be progress for all men, the leadership must come primarily from the highly industrialized nations of the free world, and can only be accomplished if those nations coordinate their own expanding economies to make a maximum effort.

This brings us to the third consideration, "the creation of a true Atlantic Community within the next decade." The phrase, "true Atlantic Community," is subject to many interpretations. The signers of the Declaration of Paris sketched out some directions in which such a community could evolve. In the following chapters I shall try to describe what has been done in efforts to bring the Atlantic Community together; what my own concept of a true Atlantic Community is; how I feel that it must be the nucleus for a broader grouping of free nations; and how I believe the development of such a concept can be advanced, step by step, during the timespan vouchsafed to us in our struggle to survive as free men.

Chapter II

Integration in Western Europe

A brief backward look at history is essential to a realization of the momentous, revolutionary changes which have taken place.

Over many centuries individuals or nations have tried to create a single state on the continent of Europe, using military conquest as an instrument for unification. This was the dream of Charlemagne and Napoleon, and more recently the nightmares visited upon the world by the Germany of Kaiser Wilhelm and of Adolf Hitler. All such efforts failed, the ambitions of individuals leading to military disaster and national defeat. World War I culminated not only in the lopsided Treaty of Versailles, but also in the creation of an unstable equilibrium of many small or newly independent states with the breakup of the Austro-Hungarian empire. President Wilson's courageous attempts to create an effective international organization to keep the peace, the League of Nations, were doomed to failure, in large measure because the United States itself refused to ratify the League Covenant. However, neither the redrawing of the boundaries of nations on the continent nor the ill-fated League of Nations was the most important outcome of World War I. More significant was the very fact of the entry of the United States into the war: it was the determination of the United States to cross the ocean and join hands with the nations of Western Europe in order to crush the German bid for domination which turned the tide of the conflict, and for the first time brought the two sides of the Atlantic Ocean close together. The significance of that fact was only partly vitiated by our relapse into isolation after the war. The second important outcome was the Russian Revolution, leading to Russia's withdrawal from the war and the creation of a Communist-dominated state as successor to the empire of the Tsars.

Up to the time of our entry into the war the United States was essentially an isolationist nation. It had followed meticulously the precepts of George Washington's Farewell Address in refusing entangling alliances with foreign powers, and had devoted itself almost exclusively to its own internal development. It had had its difficulties from time to time, even minor wars, with Britain, France, Mexico, and Spain; but these related essentially to its own security problems in the Western Hemisphere. Its refusal to take responsibility for the Versailles peace settlement or to join the League of Nations was a continuing reflex of long-established isolationist attitudes and policy.

From 1930 to 1940 we watched, with the same unfortunate detachment as the British and the French, the crumbling of the Weimar Republic and then the insidious growth and military activity of Nazi Germany. It seemed inconceivable to us that Germany could, in so short a span of time, have made a physical recovery of sufficient proportions to constitute a menace to the rest of Europe. War in Europe broke out, and we stood on the sidelines watching the occupation of France and the struggles on the Russian front, lending material aid but not ourselves becoming embroiled in the conflict although pushed by events closer and closer to it. It was the sneak attack on

Pearl Harbor by the Japanese which shook us to our roots. We soon found ourselves engaged in total war, trying not only to help save Europe and the Middle East from German conquest, but likewise forced to carry on a full-scale war with the Japanese in the Pacific.

World War II ended with a complete destruction of Japanese power as well as with the total defeat of Germany. It left both the Japanese economy and that of Europe, including European Russia, in shambles. It left the United States untouched within its borders, and with its industrial potential tremendously enhanced. The United States became the dominant power of the world, having at its disposal not only a greatly increased industrial plant but also, in its sole possession, nuclear weapons. The United Kingdom knew the nuclear secrets but did not have the plant. The Soviet Union had the potential but needed time— though less than we anticipated—to develop it.

The war did much more than this, however. It left the United States with the full realization that isolationism was a thing of the past, and that the future of the United States was inextricably bound up with every other section of the world. From this new awareness there developed the dedicated American effort to create the United Nations, with high hopes that a new and universal international organization, in which the nations which had emerged victorious from the war could take the leading role, would provide a mechanism for averting future wars and for the development of rules by which international disputes could be settled.

Along with the organization of the United Nations should be mentioned the Bretton Woods institutions—the International Monetary Fund and the International Bank for Reconstruction and Development. While these were established in 1945 technically as specialized agencies of the United Nations, the Soviet Union and most of the

Communist bloc countries declined membership or withdrew after joining, with the result that they became, in effect, agencies of the free world, with membership now of nearly seventy countries. The countries of the Atlantic Community provide their principal strength both in resources and management. Both institutions have proved themselves of immense value in the postwar economic recovery and the achievement of financial stability and growth, and in promoting economic cooperation.

Finally, if any proof were needed that America's destiny after two world wars was tied to that of Europe, the United States evolved the Marshall Plan, the boldest and most successful attempt ever made by any nation to lend its strength toward assisting the economic recovery of its friends. Perhaps the least known and appreciated decision with regard to the Marshall Plan was the insistence by the United States, under the leadership of Will Clayton, then Under Secretary of State for Economic Affairs, that the nations which would receive aid should organize among themselves an instrumentality which would make the broad determination as to where and in what amount American resources made available by the Marshall Plan should be applied. This led to the creation of the Organization for European Economic Cooperation (OEEC), first as an essentially technical group made up of experts whose findings nevertheless were virtually controlling in the administration of Marshall Plan aid, although the United States retained the power to determine how the aid was divided. While the United States did not become a member of the OEEC, it worked very closely with it and helped to assure its effectiveness.

The OEEC, in which eighteen states were represented, proved so useful that it gradually undertook a coordinated economic program of wide scope, guided by a permanent council and by periodic conferences at the ministerial level.

Its most valuable work was bringing about the reduction and finally the practical elimination of quotas as instruments of restraint on the movement of manufactured goods among European countries, and the stabilization of currencies through the medium of the European Payments Union, which not only provided currency clearing arrangements but also served as an influential advisory group on monetary and fiscal policies. From that beginning there developed the various steps leading toward a greater economic integration of Western Europe and the first discernible outlines which brought a true Atlantic Community within the realm of the possible.

In the preceding chapter I referred briefly to the events which led to the North Atlantic Treaty, an alliance essentially military and defensive in character. By establishing its own integrated command and armed forces in peacetime, however, and its institutions for continuing consultation, NATO soon became much more than an old-fashioned military alliance. The OEEC marked the beginning of a parallel effort toward the economic and political integration of Europe. In the early stages of both of these organizations there was one common factor. The United States provided the principal power tools with which NATO could become an effective military alliance; and in the case of OEEC, the United States provided the principal material assistance which, when joined with Europe's own efforts, made it possible for the component nations to rejuvenate and begin to integrate their economies.

At a later point I shall give some attention to the military problems still disturbing the NATO alliance, but before doing so I feel that a brief review of the successive steps which have been taken in Europe leading toward closer coordination from an economic as well as a political point of view would be useful, for they have played an essential part both in the growing unity of Western Europe and in the building of sentiment favoring an Atlantic Community.

Little more than a decade ago a comparatively small group of men [1] came to the conclusion that Western Europe could fulfill its own potential as a leader in the free world only through close economic integration followed by political unity. They felt that an approach primarily through functional means was the rational way to break down the obstacles of nationalism created by many centuries of national rivalries and of wars that were interrupted by only one long period of relative peace during the nineteenth century. These individuals, through the carrying power of their deep convictions and their ability to influence their respective governments, set in motion the trend which began with the creation of the European Coal and Steel Community. That organization had definite supranational features with institutions exercising control which cut across the borders of the member states. It embraced separate executive, legislative and judicial institutions. In spite of the misgivings of many who felt that such an encroachment on the sovereignty of the individual member states could not last long, it proved highly successful. Great Britain, though asked to join the Coal and Steel Community, held off, still motivated by its long-held policy of remaining aloof from such close involvement in the internal problems of the continent.

The Coal and Steel Community became the prototype for the next two developments, the creation of the European Atomic Energy Community (EURATOM) and the European Economic Community (EEC), generally called the Common Market. EURATOM followed very closely the functional lines of the Coal and Steel Community in addressing itself to a segment of the economy of the same group of nations. It again created a supranational author-

[1] Most prominent among these were Monnet, Schuman and Pleven of France, Spaak of Belgium, De Gasperi of Italy, and Adenauer of Germany.

ity to develop among the member nations the uses of atomic energy for peaceful purposes. Its actual development has been slow; but it is a step forward that parts of its institutional structure—the Assembly and the Court, as is also the case with the Coal and Steel Community—have been merged with those of EEC.

The EEC is a much more revolutionary development than either the Coal and Steel Community or EURATOM. Its eventual impact on the whole world will not be measured for many years to come, but its early successes and its influence in forcing the other great industrial nations of the free world to review their own policies indicate the profound nature of its initial impact. For this reason, it is necessary to examine briefly its structure and the progress which it has made in its four years of existence.

The basic document creating the EEC is the Treaty of Rome, signed by France, the Federal Republic of Germany, Italy, Holland, Belgium and Luxembourg in 1957. It was ratified that same year by each of those nations, and the provisions for the first stage of its operation became effective on January 1, 1958. The treaty itself is a voluminous document of some 248 separate articles plus annexes, protocols, conventions and declarations. It creates four principal institutions for the effective carrying-out of its purposes, as well as a number of subsidiary bodies formed for special purposes. The four institutional bodies are: first, a Commission, which proposes community policy and has day-to-day administrative authority; second, a Council of Ministers, which decides community policy and has prime executive responsibility; third, an Assembly, which serves as a limited parliament; fourth, a Court of Justice, which passes judgment on legal issues arising under the treaty.

The Commission is made up of persons of "general competence" and "unquestioned integrity," selected by agreement of the member governments and acting not as representatives of their nations but as servants of the whole community. In some matters it is given independent powers of decision, while on others its function is to make proposals and recommendations, their confirmation resting with the Council. In the initial stages provided in the treaty the Council, composed of ministers representing the respective states, acts on important matters, including all proposals made by the Commission, like any such international body requiring the agreement of all for its decisions, with the power of veto in the hands of any one nation. As time goes on and the further stages provided for by the treaty are reached, the Council operates more and more without the power of veto resting in a single nation and must make decisions by weighted or qualified votes. The Treaty of Rome specifies which type of vote is required for different types of decisions; and once a vote has been taken, it is binding upon all the nations signatory to the treaty.[2] Thus the supranational character of the community grows as it passes through the transition stages to the goal of economic union.

The EEC Assembly, the members of which are designated by the parliaments of each government, has, as of now, only recommendatory powers; but it can, by a two-thirds vote of its members, require the Commission to resign, after which new Commissioners would be chosen by the member governments. Looking to the future, the Treaty of Rome provided that the Assembly should draw up proposals for election of its members by direct popular vote instead of their being appointed by the various national parliaments.

[2] In such voting the respective nations are given the following figures: France, 4; Germany, 4; Italy, 4; Holland, 2; Belgium, 2; Luxembourg, 1. In some matters the prescribed majority is 12; in others, 12 votes representing a favorable vote by at least four members.

The last important institutional body set up is the Court, which has full jurisdiction to pass upon any disputes arising under the provisions of the Treaty of Rome. Its decisions are final.

The Treaty of Rome provided a schedule for the reduction of internal tariffs by stages, pledged in advance by the member nations. It was contemplated that this would be done in steps of 10 per cent, across-the-board reductions, culminating in 1972 in a complete abolition of all tariffs with respect to the trade of these nations among themselves. As of today these internal reductions have taken place with much greater rapidity than was originally contemplated, and already a 50 per cent reduction on industrial goods has been accomplished.

The treaty likewise provided for a common external tariff for the six member nations. With some exceptions it was to be determined by computing the average in each category of goods of the 1957 tariffs of each nation. This common external tariff can be altered only by the action of the Commission or Council.

The treaty further provided for the free movement of capital, services and labor among the member countries; and made a number of provisions for the control of cartels, the elimination of quantitative restrictions or quotas on trade, and the creation of special development funds for less developed regions within the Community and associated overseas countries and territories. In other words, the Treaty of Rome envisaged the integration of the respective economies of the member nations far beyond the scope of a customs union.

There was one additional provision in the Treaty of Rome that should be mentioned. It provided for measures of assistance to industries injured by the progressive reduction of internal tariffs which require re-employment or retraining for their workers or monetary compensation for their losses. Because of the full employment in these nations and the consequent easy shifting of industries and workers to the production of other goods, adjustment assistance has not been called for in the treaty, although there has been such assistance in the Coal and Steel Community, notably for some high-cost coal mines in Belgium.

Many figures could be cited to show the great initial success of the Common Market and the changing attitude of many industrialists in Europe toward the benefits of the internal tariff reductions which have taken place. Suffice it to say that this is a major reason why production in these nations has risen faster than any in Western Europe, and the rate of growth has been approximately twice that of the United States. These initial successes have led the EEC to accelerate the program envisaged in the Treaty of Rome to a rate which may well reduce the internal tariffs to the vanishing point by 1967.

Any nation in Europe, according to the treaty, may apply for admission to the Common Market. Whether it would expand beyond the original six members depended largely on the decision to be taken by Europe's greatest trading nation, Great Britain. The British refused the invitation to membership initially offered to them, for two principal reasons. First, the Treaty of Rome provided that all members must become a part of its institutional structure and foreshadowed growing political ties that meant some sacrifice of national sovereignty. The second was the difficulty in reconciling a common external tariff, as required by the EEC, with the long-established preferences given by Britain to its associated nations in the Commonwealth. Up until 1959 the British felt that they could negotiate some kind of free-trade-area arrangement which would allow them to get the benefit of the Common Market and retain their special arrangements with the Commonwealth nations.

When those negotiations broke down, the British organized a rival organization. Austria, Switzerland, Portugal, Denmark, Norway and Sweden joined them in an association called the European Free Trade Association (EFTA), which, like the Common Market, would progressively reduce tariffs among its members but, unlike the Common Market, left each nation free to fix its own external tariff. This group has reduced the tariffs among its members by percentages equivalent to those achieved in the Common Market. But the device of EFTA, intended less as a permanent arrangement than as a counter for bargaining with the EEC for a unified free trade area, did not provide the key to Britain's own future in the face of the growing economic unity of Europe. Consequently the British government concluded that the logical and statesmanlike course was to apply for membership in the EEC.

As of the moment that these lines are written, the entry of Great Britain into the Common Market is still uncertain. In my judgment, however, the chances in favor of admission outweigh those against, although our planning should not lose sight of the possibility that Great Britain's entry may be blocked. The experience which Great Britain has gone through since its request for admission is, moreover, of some interest and importance to the United States, if merely because the day will soon be approaching when we shall be negotiating for some form of trade partnership with the Common Market.

In Great Britain the Macmillan government, having made up its mind to apply for membership, decided to throw its whole weight and its whole political future into the scales. Despite the opposition of a wing of the Conservative party which includes at least thirty members of Parliament and assuming the total opposition of the Labour party—an assumption which is not fully justified as of this moment, since a group within the Labour party has already taken a position favorable to joining and a final party position has not been taken—the government seems to have the votes to ratify accession on the best terms that can be obtained in negotiations with the six.

The relationship of Great Britain to the Commonwealth during the recent discussions has been most revealing. The principal objections to British membership in the Common Market at the Commonwealth Conference held in England in September 1962 came from the "old" Dominions of Canada, Australia and New Zealand, although real anxiety was shown also by a number of the Asian members of the Commonwealth. The leaders of Canada and Australia expressed their dissent in no uncertain terms. After numerous discussions, however, the Commonwealth nations all "took note of the considerations which had influenced the British Government in deciding to accede to the European Economic Community if satisfactory terms could be secured," and recognized that "the responsibility for the final decision would rest with the British Government." [3]

In the case of Canada, Australia and New Zealand, the anxieties revolved largely around the preferred position which agricultural exports from those countries hold in the British market. It was with respect to these exports that the British government has done its best to obtain for them as favorable a position as possible in its negotiations with representatives of the Common Market countries, and has not been wholly successful. Once again, it was a clear-cut demonstration that the treatment of agricultural products was the stickiest with which the Common Market countries had to contend among themselves, with which the British had to cope internally in Great Britain,

[3] *The Times* (London), September 20, 1962.

with which the Commonwealth nations had to deal, and with which, in the future, the United States is likely to be most concerned. However, as I indicated above, I am optimistic that in time these agricultural problems will be resolved and that they will not present an insuperable obstacle to Great Britain's becoming a full member of the Common Market.

My optimism was greater earlier than it is now, only because of the recent curious attitude displayed by General de Gaulle and Chancellor Adenauer with respect to the admission of Great Britain. The British have made it clear that they would accept all the political implications of the Treaty of Rome and work as a full member of the EEC toward greater political unification. From the statements made in Paris and Bonn, there are indications that General de Gaulle and Chancellor Adenauer would prefer to work out political arrangements for the Common Market countries without Great Britain and are, therefore, inclined to put continuing obstacles in the way of British admission. It is not merely with the British themselves that the decision lies.

Earlier I mentioned the fact that the creation of EEC was a revolutionary thing. Over a short span of years it will bring into existence a free-trade or nearly free-trade area consisting of from two to three hundred million persons, depending upon how many other European nations decide to join its ranks. In population this would constitute a free trade area larger than that of the United States. This area would allow the development of mass production, healthy competition, modern marketing techniques and other practices such as have never been known in Europe before, in turn leading to a vastly increased productivity on the continent.

While other nations in Europe have applied for admission to the Common Market, with action deferred until the question of British admission is settled, British membership in the Market is nevertheless likely to play an extremely important part in our own deliberations and the form which our partnership may take. Two American administrations have strongly favored British membership, a fact which unfortunately has been stressed from time to time by the Common Market's opponents in Great Britain. This support is entirely logical if one favors a closer relationship among the nations of the Atlantic Community, since the British are clearly a major link between the two sides of the Atlantic; not alone because of language and racial ties, but because of the very close relationship between Canada and Great Britain. Should it happen that the British do not come into the EEC, I would think it almost inevitable that a new combination of some type like EFTA would develop and that our own position would become greatly complicated. The situation obviously would be quite different. Nevertheless, the need for a closely associated Atlantic Community including Western Europe, Britain and the United States would remain. If it were not an integral part of a European union, Britain would still seek, perhaps all the more avidly, a place in the broader Atlantic association.

The progressive association of the United States with a Europe that is growing in strength and in unity may take place through existing organizations, or perhaps might require new ones. Both EEC and EFTA are European organizations. NATO, on the other hand, which includes both the United States and Canada, is an Atlantic Community organization. While the general concept of NATO is military and political, nevertheless, under Article II of its Charter, provision was made for an expansion of activities and authority in the economic field.[4] In spite of the efforts of former Secretary General Spaak, NATO has not implemented Article II. Instead, a separate economic organization, a successor to OEEC, was created and became operative in October 1961—the Organization for Economic Cooperation and Development (OECD). This organization embraces not only the nations which belonged to OEEC, including five non-NATO nations (Sweden, Austria, Switzerland, Spain and Ireland), but also the United States and Canada. Membership in OECD carries very limited obligations. It is essentially a consultative and recommendatory body. Its purpose is to assist in coordinating its members' economic and fiscal policies as well as to develop plans for effective coordinated action in the field of assistance to the less developed nations. It is difficult to foresee how important an instrument it may become in the development of the Atlantic Community. This will depend on whether its members try positively to use it as a means of common action. It has great potentials, not only as an organization in which both sides of the Atlantic are represented, but because it has brought Japan into its deliberations connected with the development of foreign aid programs.

If OECD does not grow and develop as a vigorous Atlantic institution, there may be new forms and relationships which will tie the United States more closely to Europe, more particularly to the Common Market. Under legislation recently adopted the United States is trying to

4 "The Parties will contribute toward the further development of peaceful and friendly international relations by strengthening their free institutions, by bringing about a better understanding of the principles upon which these institutions are founded, and by promoting conditions of stability and well-being. They will seek to eliminate conflict in their international economic policies and will encourage economic collaboration between any or all of them."

create an effective trade partnership with the EEC. The outlines of such a partnership are not yet clear, nor is the final structure of EEC, as several European nations are still negotiating for membership or associated status. Certain broad outlines are clearly discernible however. The free trade area of the EEC in Europe is likely to be greatly expanded; and continuing efforts toward the creation of the United States of Europe, the dream envisaged by those who are principally responsible for the signing of the Treaty of Rome, are making steady though slow progress.

This question of how the political unity of Europe should be achieved is a crucial one for Great Britain, and even more so for the United States as it contemplates its own relationship to Europe. At the moment it is difficult for these two nations to see what alternatives lie before them so long as sharp differences of view still exist among the EEC nations themselves and there is no agreement on the nature of the association which other European nations, including the traditional neutrals, will have with them.

General de Gaulle foresees a loose confederation of nations with each nation retaining complete freedom of action while pledging itself to consultation and coordination. Other nations, with Belgium and Holland in the lead, are advocating a much tighter federation in which each nation would cede to supranational institutions some of its sovereignty. Italy appears to lean to that same view. Chancellor Adenauer favors it also, although he does not wish to do anything to disturb the present close association between Germany and France. Many leading figures in Germany would go beyond Europe geographically and have expressed the conviction that a federation should embrace not only European nations but also the United States and Canada as essential elements in combining the military and economic strength of the two sides of the Atlantic.

Much of the talk on the political side is still vague. But it is necessary for Americans to take it into account, and to form their own ideas on the larger aspects of European unity and Atlantic unity as their government goes about the practical business of defining its relations with those organizations that have already come into being, particularly the dynamic entity known as the European Common Market.

Chapter III

Roads to Union

The development of a true Atlantic Community may take several directions. Moving concurrently, there are three separate lines of association which may or may not ultimately converge. The first is that in which, thus far, the European nations alone are concerned. The second, in the NATO context, is that in which a group of European nations, together with the United States and Canada, have built an alliance which is primarily military but has political ties as well. The third is that in which nearly all the European nations, plus the United States and Canada, are moving toward closer economic ties. Closely allied with these three is the important policy question of the relationship of Europe and the Atlantic Community to Japan, to the British Commonwealth countries, and to the less developed and uncommitted nations of the rest of the world.

In Europe the dynamism of the EEC is apparent. But vital questions are still unanswered. Will its membership go beyond the original six countries? What political shape will it take? The prospects for a true Atlantic Community will depend on the answers Europe gives to these questions. Within the EEC, as we have seen, substantial divergencies already exist in the matter of closer political ties. If Britain joins, there will be still another viewpoint, probably one which is very leery of supranational institutions and real political unity.

There is no more difficult speculation than trying to visualize the institutional framework which may effectively bring political unity to Europe, for sharp differences exist within as well as between nations. It is particularly true when one appreciates the fact that General de Gaulle has his own strong personal views favoring a loose confederation with no really supranational institutional ties whatever while, on the other hand, a very substantial majority of persons important in French political life believe, as do the Germans, that strong supranational ties are essential.

In each of the European countries there is a school of opinion, at times quite vocal, which is interested in the political unification of Europe in order that Europe may become a third force, holding place with the United States and Russia in the determination of world policy. This opinion is strengthened by the unhappy feeling of frustration which many Europeans feel arising from their continuing dependence on the United States from a military standpoint. It rests on the conviction that a unified Europe could greatly lessen this dependence and would even allow Europe, if it saw fit, to adopt a middle-ground or neutralist attitude between the more belligerent positions of the Soviet bloc and the United States. Encouragement of this line of thinking carries real dangers of breaking the military alliance and the unity of policy so essential to our survival. Fortunately, most leaders in Europe are conscious of this danger.

The policies which the United States itself may adopt will surely influence the final outcome of this conflict of views and the forms which the European movement toward greater unity will take. At the moment, with Great Britain's relationship to the continental nations still unclear, the question of American policies on political unification is not immediately posed. It would appear from statements made by administration leaders that our government is committed to the proposition that Europe should first consolidate effectively before consideration can be given to a larger Atlantic unity. There are many on this side and a few in Europe who contend that European unity should be achieved within the framework of Atlantic institutions. I am personally inclined to the belief that it is futile to insist upon Atlantic political unity until the European nations, themselves, have determined the degree to which they are willing to federate. Political unity, for the moment, appears vaguely remote, while the question of economic relations with the Common Market is before us right now. How we respond to it is of great importance in keeping open the larger questions involving the future relationship between Europe and America. It is appropriate to analyze present policy alternatives, and we must keep in mind their relation to the broader issues.

The proposals advanced by the Kennedy administration with respect to trade partnership with the EEC are, in my opinion, soundly grounded. They do, however, involve difficulties which may make an effective partnership impossible. The first of these springs from our own governmental structure in which, by the separation of powers between the legislative and executive branches, agreements in the field of trade are continually subject to review by the legislative branch. Under our Constitution, Congress has very broad powers in the control of tariffs. Just how far it will, in the long run, be willing to delegate its powers to the executive is still an open question; and it may well be that the executive will have to try to make the necessary international arrangements on trade in the form of treaties rather than executive agreements. In that event, ratification by a two-thirds vote of the Senate will be required.

The second difficulty lies in the inclusion in the trade bill of an escape clause provision, sponsored by the administration, whereby the United States would retain the right by unilateral action to raise tariffs or impose quotas in order to protect certain segments of our economy from outside competition.

The third difficulty lies in our own apparent inability to develop a rational agricultural policy whereby our production can be kept within manageable limits, and whereby the disposal of surpluses through sale or gift can be so coordinated with the agricultural policies of other nations so as to minimize the frictions only too apparent in this field.

The fourth difficulty relates to the administration's insistence, in which I fully concur, that any trade partnership which we conclude with Europe and which has as its principal objective the reduction of tariffs, should extend the benefits of such reductions to all other qualified nations in the world who wish to adjust their trade policies accordingly.

Agreement may well be reached and domestic policy adjusted so as to make some of the difficulties now facing us more manageable. However, there should be no glossing over certain unpleasant facts. The United States has imposed certain tariff and quota restrictions on lead and zinc and oil. In the cases of lead and zinc, there are pressures to maintain in operation many small, high-cost, producing mines in the United States. With respect to oil, our restrictive policy was dictated not alone by the domestic oil producers in this country, but also by the coal producers who were having difficulty in competing with imports of so-called residual oil products, largely from Venezuela, which have been used as a substitute for coal. These restrictions have been particularly burdensome on certain nations of Latin America, such as Venezuela and Peru, whose economy we have been trying to assist through vast aid programs.

The United States has engaged in other practices, particularly in the agricultural field, which complicate greatly the establishment of an effective Atlantic partnership. In the case of sugar, it has established import quotas which arbitrarily allocate to certain countries a specified amount of sugar which they can ship into the United States and for which they are paid a premium price. These quotas make for a substantial subsidy to the favored countries, which receive almost double the price of sugar in the world market. Cuba was the principal beneficiary in days gone by. It is no longer. Today the United States selects the beneficiaries as it sees fit. This policy of limiting our imports of sugar was adopted in order to maintain an artificially high price in this country for the benefit of domestic cane and beet sugar producers.

We have also subsidized cotton producers of this country by maintaining a high support price, at the same time offering a bounty on surplus cotton for export of approximately eight and one-half cents per pound. As a result, the United States sells cotton to all other nations at a cheaper price than its own textile industry can purchase cotton. This is, in effect, an overseas dumping policy, but one which puts our own textile industry at the serious disadvantage of having to pay more for American produced cotton than do its principal rivals overseas.

Today, through mechanization and better technology with regard to both seed and planting, and through the greatly increased use of fertilizer the United States can produce wheat and corn as cheaply as any nation in the world. And yet we maintain artificially high prices for these basic grains with resulting unmanageable surpluses. Here again our policies have stemmed from an effort to protect the small and uneconomical farmer. We have not fully realized that farming in this country has become a large-scale industry in which the capital investment required to produce a livelihood for a single individual is considerably greater than the amount of capital required in industry for the same purpose.

I have cited these examples only because they represent important obstacles in the path to an effective trade partnership.

Agriculture, largely because of the political influence and social desirability of the small independent farmer, has special problems for nearly every nation. Within the EEC itself, agriculture has posed some of the knottiest problems which have not yet been fully resolved. The problems may, in fact, be complicated further by Great Britain's application for membership in the Common Market, because of her pledges to her own farmers and her effort to protect the preferential arrangements which she has made for farm products with her Commonwealth associates. So difficult are these farm problems that they may have to be handled by a separate type of negotiation in which world-wide commodity agreements would be separated from ordinary tariff agreements on manufactured products. Already some headway has been made in this direction.

The second of the converging lines toward the development of a true Atlantic Community is the military. NATO is a military alliance born of a common military threat. Although, as previously noted, its membership includes two nations of the Eastern Mediteranean, Greece and Turkey, it represents primarily the preponderant power of Western Europe and North America. As a military alliance it will probably last as long as the common military threat exists. Unlike military alliances of the past, it has a structure which permits of almost continuous consultation and coordination among special ambassadors of the member nations sitting in Paris. It also provides in its Charter for the development of economic cooperation, although with the formation of OECD this provision has not been resorted to.

In spite of being essentially a military alliance, NATO has had great political influence. It has maintained necessary and useful solidarity in peacetime and has proved in many ways an effective piece of machinery, inducing the habit of coordinating policies and building common policies and institutions. Without NATO and without its effectiveness as a military alliance, talks of European or Atlantic unity are futile. To many, NATO appears to be a unified structure on the continent of Europe with an American commander in chief. Its unity of direction for military purposes seems to make it a solid bastion against aggression from the Soviet block. This concept, while partly true, does not reveal some of the underlying weaknesses besetting the alliance—weaknesses arising largely from the preponderant strength of the United States in relation to that of the other partners.

From the outset NATO has had two separate command structures with certain subordinated commands coordinated by a standing group of three military officers (British, French and American) located in Washington. SACEUR (Supreme Allied Command, Europe), with headquarters in Paris, has since its inception been led by four American military officers, General Eisenhower, General Ridgway, General Gruenther and General Norstad. There has likewise been a second command structure known as SACLANT (Supreme Allied Command, Atlantic), with headquarters in Norfolk, Virginia. Few Americans realize that on American soil there is the largest naval base in the world, dedicated not to the defense of the United States alone, but to the defense of the interests of all the NATO countries in the Atlantic. In both of these commands there are representatives of the military establishments of various NATO nations, and even though at present they are headed by U.S. officers, nonetheless they are essentially international in character. There is, in addition, a Channel Command, under British commanders, with responsibility for defense of the English Channel and southern part of the North Sea.

In Europe the command has certain subdivisions. There is the command of the Mediterranean fleet, the reponsibilities of which are confined to that sea. On the continent there are Allied commanders for Northern, Central, and Southern Europe, whose responsibilities embrace appropriate ground, air, and naval forces of the respective nations. All of these subordinate commands are under SACEUR. With regard to the troops on the continent, although they are under international command, they are nevertheless grouped in separate national units, most of them equipped with such arms as are deemed most appropriate by the separate nations. The only complete coordination among them in time of peace comes in what is known as the infrastructure, which is financed by funds levied by the separate nations after budgetary agreement in the NATO Council. This infrastructure is made up of common air bases, logistical facilities and communications.

All the military units assigned to the NATO command have as their primary responsibility the defense of the NATO alliance, wherein an attack on one nation is considered an attack on all. West Berlin is included in the area covered by the NATO guarantee. Each NATO nation, however, has reserved to itself the right in the event of an emergency affecting itself to withdraw its own units, temporarily at least, for use elsewhere in that emergency. For example, the majority of the French troops which in recent years were utilized in Algeria were originally assigned to the NATO shield in Western Europe and were withdrawn by the French, without replacement, for use in Algeria. This was not strictly a withdrawal from NATO since much of Algeria was considered by France to be an integral part of metropolitan France, and as such was specifically covered by the NATO guarantee. Nevertheless, the decision to move French troops to Algeria was made unilaterally by France. Similarly, when the United States sent a contingent of troops to Lebanon, these were taken from its units stationed in Germany and from the Sixth Fleet operating under the Mediterranean command. Again, the decision to utilize these troops outside of the NATO area was made unilaterally by the United States. Three years ago the French decided to withdraw their naval units from the Mediterranean command and to reconstitute them as an independent French naval unit. This was done by the unilateral decision of the French government, even though it stated at the same time that these units would be returned to the Mediterranean command in the event of war.

The greatest difficulty in achieving effective unity of command has resulted from the existence of nuclear weapons. When the Atlantic alliance was formed, the United States alone had a nuclear capability. Its strategic strength in this field became the principal arm of the alliance. Great Britain developed nuclear weapons shortly after the United States, and since 1958 the United States has assisted the British nuclear program. But in 1949 the West's monopoly was lost as Soviet Russia produced fission and later fusion weapons. Today, mutual destruction might well be the result of an all-out nuclear war. Hence, decisions on whether or not nuclear weapons should be used under varying conditions becomes a matter of paramount importance to all members of the alliance.

How would the decision be made to use nuclear weapons

now deployed in Europe? Under the Atomic Energy Act of 1946, as amended, the United States cannot share its nuclear weapons technology with an ally which has not already developed a nuclear capability. Britain qualified for assistance. France asked for similar assistance. In view of strong American policy against further diffusion of nuclear weapons production capabilities, and France's policy of minimal cooperation with NATO, it appears likely that she will not soon receive American assistance in producing nuclear weapons. None of the other countries of the alliance has made any serious effort to develop them.

Custody of nuclear weapons deployed overseas for wartime use by our allies must, by U.S. law, remain in peacetime in U.S. hands. The release of nuclear weapons, whether they are stationed with NATO troops in Europe or are in the United States or in Polaris submarines, is dependent upon a decision by the President of the United States. The British have a power of decision with respect to nuclear weapons of their own manufacture.

This tremendous power of decision left to the United States has created serious problems for NATO. Some doubt has arisen in the minds of Europeans as to whether their interests are best served by this arrangement. These doubts spring from three causes. The first is that we might get involved in a war, let us say in Southeast Asia, which would quickly lead to the use of nuclear weapons on Chinese targets, to be followed in turn by the use by Russia, as China's ally, of nuclear weapons against the U.S. Seventh Fleet, our installations in Okinawa and Japan, or on the United States itself. Should a war of this kind develop, in the start of which our European allies had no voice, they fear that it would automatically engulf Europe through its inevitable escalation to general nuclear warfare.

Their second doubt arises from their fear that if an attack were made by the Russians on a European NATO ally, the United States, fearful of an all-out nuclear war, would hesitate to utilize its nuclear power in coming to the assistance of that nation. The third doubt comes from the possibility of an attack from the Soviet bloc on one of the NATO nations, limited to non-nuclear weapons, thus leaving to the United States alone the decision whether to respond with nuclear weapons.

These various doubts are inconsistent. They are, nevertheless, real. They point up the desirability of finding some formula for reassuring our allies that their counsels and concerns will be given full consideration. The problem also involves finding an acceptable command structure and a way of meeting certain contingencies at a time in history when decisions may not be possible through the ordinary processes of consultation since the time element involved in any surprise attack may be one of minutes rather than days.

In recognition of these factors the United States has taken a number of important steps to try to meet the legitimate concern of its allies as far as it can be done consistent with our national policy of limiting the spread of nuclear secrets. In 1957, at the December meeting of heads of government in Paris, President Eisenhower offered to establish in Europe NATO stockpiles of nuclear warheads. The proposal was that these stockpiles would be established in every area where there were planes, guns, or missiles capable of carrying nuclear warheads, either in the hands of U.S. or other NATO forces. Thus, in case of attack the warheads could be furnished to the carriers. Allied forces were trained in the use and means of transferring the warheads. The whole process was subject to intergovernmental agreements laid in each case before Congress before they became effective.

This plan was accepted and has been widely put into effect. Thus, we and the allied forces have nuclear-capable planes, guns, or missiles (of short or long range) which can be used promptly if needed.[1] These weapons are under the NATO command, but their use would require also the consent of the governments of the United States and of the other nations concerned.

The sharing of decisions in nuclear matters has been carried further. The NATO Council is being kept informed of the general deposition and plans of nuclear forces. Even the targeting of nuclear weapons in the NATO command is in the charge of an international staff.

More important than these technical arrangements is the agreement of the NATO allies to consult with each other with regard to any situations in which trouble may be threatened. This is the stage, after all, where policies may be influenced. When the trigger actually has to be pulled, it is usually too late to consult.

We have also devoted much time and energy to exploring the possibilities for a nuclear striking force that would be clearly under NATO command and control. At the ministerial meeting of NATO in December 1960 I advanced a concept for at least a partial solution for the United States. A firm proposal could not be made since that meeting was held after election day and before the newly elected administration had taken over. The concept was that the United States would commit to NATO five submarines carrying a total of eighty Polaris missiles. If our allies provided additional missiles on a multilaterally manned, owned, and controlled basis, deployed either in submarines, in surface vessels, or on land, the United States would then combine its five submarines with the contribution made by our allies into a NATO deterrent force under NATO command. How the NATO command

[1] France, however, has refused to allow stockpiles on her soil, but has recently, in conformity with the 1957 agreement, given assent to stock-piling to supply the French troops stationed in Germany.

should be constituted was left for subsequent consideration.

In May 1961 President Kennedy reaffirmed this concept in a public speech, but dropped out the requirement that our allies should themselves provide a counterpart to the five Polaris submarines which we were willing to offer to a NATO command, adding the condition that our allies should strengthen their conventional forces. At Athens in May 1962 the United States formally made this offer, but without any conditions.

The objective of the United States in offering this concept was twofold. The first was to create a nuclear capability under NATO command. In simpler terms, it made of NATO, as a collective unit, the fourth effective nuclear power. Second was the hope that the creation of a NATO nuclear deterrent would lead the French to abandon their efforts to become a separate nuclear power, and so in turn discourage other Western European nations from seeking the same goal. The plan was not intended to be a total answer to the problem of Europe's defense. Our European allies must come to realize that as NATO itself builds a nuclear force, of which the Soviet Union must take account in deciding its own strategy, it does not thereby avoid the need for increased non-nuclear forces.

As yet, there has been no effective response from the European nations. Neither there nor here has an acceptable solution of the problem of control over nuclear forces been found. In my opinion this remains a question of the highest priority for the NATO alliance. Because it touches the vital matters of sovereignty and national security of the members, it is bound to be difficult to solve. But for the same reason it is an essential key to the development of an Atlantic Community.

The third converging line of policy toward Atlantic unity is that envisaging an economic development in which the European nations, together with the United States and Canada, would develop a trade partnership. Such a trade partnership has been referred to on numerous occasions by the Kennedy administration as a most important goal. The position of Canada will depend, in large measure, on the outcome of the negotiations between the United Kingdom and the European Economic Community with regard to British membership in the Common Market. However, should the United States be successful in negotiating a real trade partnership with the Common Market, I think Canada would follow a similar policy.

The partnership would establish a mutually profitable working relationship between the great trade area of the fifty states in our Union and the even greater trade area, in terms of population, contained in the Common Market. This will mean reciprocal reductions in external tariffs on a gradual basis to permit the greatest possible freeing of trade between these two immense markets. While the objective appears comparatively simple, reaching it will not be easy. The current labor costs are greatly to Europe's advantage. American labor rates average nearly three times as much as those of Europe. Nor is this the whole story. Many other factors are involved in the cost of production of goods—the cost of raw materials, the cost of capital, the productivity of labor. There are also such things as reliability of delivery, merchandising skills, transportation costs and other factors, all of which must be calculated together in order to determine relative competitive positions. In these cost areas, the advantage may well lie with the United States.

Our exports exceed imports by the wide margin of approximately $5 billion annually. While agricultural products make up the largest component of total exports, we are also in a good competitive position in many lines of manufactured products. How long we can hold this position is a question which naturally arises, especially in the minds of the members of the Congress, for they are essential partners with the President in the determination of U.S. tariff policy.

The industrial recovery of Europe is based in large part on modern industrial equipment. The techniques of mass production are evolving quickly and will accelerate as the larger free trade area within the Common Market expands with the progressive reduction of internal tariffs. Europe is producing at full capacity, and there is a minimum of unemployment. European demand for both consumer goods and durable goods is very great, although still far below similar levels in the United States. Wages in Europe are increasing at a faster rate than they are in the United States, although the spread is still very great. Should Europe develop a considerable productive capacity in excess of its own internal needs, the relatively favorable export position of the United States may well be impaired.

The development of a trade partnership between the United States and the Common Market will not be easy to achieve, nor if it is achieved will we be able to hold our own competitive position without increased efforts. We will have to bring under control the continuing spiral of rising prices, and this means greater responsibility of labor unions in their demands for higher wages which, unless geared to a corresponding increase in the productivity of labor, can only lead to continually higher prices. The business community likewise must gear itself to increased competition. We shall have to use all of our ingenuity and powers of innovation in order to take full advantage of the technological improvements of which we are capable. Somewhat painful adjustments are inevitable. No matter how effective may be the adjustment assistance which Congress has provided in the current trade legislation, we must be prepared nonetheless for a certain degree of sacrifice.

Apart from the element of foreign competition, the economy of the United States is going through continuing adjustments arising from technological changes and internal competitive factors. Let me illustrate by two examples in our recent history.

While I was Governor of Massachusetts the movement of the textile industry away from New England to the southern states was in full swing. In Massachusetts there were four cities of roughly one hundred thousand population, each of whose economic life had been built around the textile industry—Lawrence, Lowell, Fall River, and New Bedford. As one textile manufacturer after another moved out of these cities to relocate in one of the southern states, unemployment became very severe. The economic plight of the cities was most serious. The movement to the South was based on comparatively simple economic considerations. A hundred years ago New England began developing a textile industry as a result of a combination of factors: some capital accumulation among its citizens, a strong pioneering spirit, but most important was that New England had many fast-running rivers which could turn mill wheels, and clean water in those rivers which was essential for scouring and dyeing. It was economical to build plants on these rivers and to bring to New England raw materials, in particular wool and cotton, from long distances. With changes in technology and with the increasing mobility of capital, the unusual advantages of New England as a textile center disappeared. Other forms of energy displaced the water of our rivers; dyeing and scouring processes were no longer dependent upon clean water. Proximity to raw materials became a large factor. In addition, labor costs on the whole were lower in the South than in New England. It was a combination of all these factors which led to this great shift in the location of our textile industry.

The problem facing the New Englanders was that of adjusting to a new situation. They did adjust, and they did so largely without governmental assistance. It was through their ingenuity and energy that they developed many new industries, some in the electronics field, some in the small-tool industry. Today, a number of the great textile plants which were idle and deserted ten years ago house as many as twenty new industries. The diversification of these new industries and the skilled labor which they require have proven to be a positive asset for the area. On balance, New England has gained. Nevertheless, there is no discounting the fact that the transitional period brought with it real hardships.

The second example is in a different field—the production of cotton. In 1940, 86 per cent of the cotton produced in this country was grown in the area stretching from the Atlantic coast across into Texas. Today that figure has been reduced to 56 per cent; 44 per cent of our cotton is produced in west Texas, Arizona, New Mexico and California. In fact, California is the greatest cotton producer in the United States. Such a shift in a comparatively brief space of time required many readjustments. In states such as South Carolina, Georgia, Mississippi and Alabama, much of the cotton was grown on small farms where individual landholders produced four to ten bales of cotton a year. These farmers are, in large measure, out of business today because this small-scale production was uneconomical and could not compete with the larger-scale production on land which was being rapidly put under irrigation in the West. These farmers have had to find other employment. Most have moved into industries or service trades. It was not foreign competition which caused these shifts, but rather technological changes within our own free trade area. The adjustment problem ascribable to potential increases in imports cannot possibly be a large one from a national standpoint, for the total of our imports amounts to less than 4 per cent of the gross national product, and tariff-protected imports constitute only 60 per cent of that total. And the new Trade Expansion Act provides a large measure of adjustment relief.

Any discussion of changes within our own economy must take into account that domestic troubles brought about by normal competitive factors have a very different political significance from those which may occur as a result of foreign competition and of governmental action in the development of an international trade partnership. A governmental act leading to injury to a given industry cannot be undertaken lightly. It must be clear that the national interest is served, and that a degree of sacrifice is required in order to attain a greater good for the country. Here the matter of adjustment assistance becomes important, and while existing legislation makes provision for such assistance in a number of different ways, I am still convinced that the adjustment which we will have to face will be made successful more by the initiative of individuals than by any form of governmental action.

The international trade partnership between the United States and Europe which is contemplated is going to take some time to create. It will require that certain actions be taken at home without delay, such as recommendations by the Tariff Commission, before we get into the actual negotiations on specific products, which will be difficult and probably protracted. I think that we may have assumed a little too lightly that the establishment of a trade partnership with the European Common Market will be easily accomplished, and that the opening up of our markets by reciprocal reductions in barriers will be so attractive to the Common Market that we in turn will be able to bargain on favorable terms. There is a strong current of opinion in Europe that the Common Market can make sufficient progress within its own area while retaining a comparatively high tariff wall around its boundaries. If that opinion predominates, as it well could, then our bargaining power may be seriously reduced. Nevertheless, the effort must be made. The alternative—two large free trade areas, both with high tariff walls and probably engaged in virtual trade war—would quickly have serious repercussions in the political field. It would gravely weaken the ability of the great industrial nations to increase their prosperity. It would substantially reduce their ability to assist less developed countries of the world, which would find their trade shut out of both areas. Worst of all, it would dash the growing hope for the creation of an Atlantic Community.

Chapter IV

Atlantic World and Free World

There is a possible fourth line of policy which might well converge with those discussed in Chapter III if an Atlantic Community is to become a reality. It lies entirely outside the Atlantic area. The Kennedy administration has made clear that any arrangement with the European Common Market would have to include extension of "most favored nation" treatment, to which we have been committed in the past. This means that reciprocal reductions in tariffs or other trade barriers would have to be made applicable to all other nations which are contracting parties to the General Agreement on Tariffs and Trade (GATT), or have bilateral "most favored nation" treaties with us, and which are willing to assume similar reciprocal obligations. The result would be a freer entry of goods from all the nations outside the Communist bloc into the markets of the United States and Europe. The implications are very great.

Japan, with over ninety millions of people, has made an industrial recovery perhaps even more extraordinary than that of Western Europe. It is by far the strongest industrial country in the Far East. It has shifted its prewar trade patterns radically. Much of its raw materials and a considerable part of its food then came from Manchuria and China, and a good part of its trade was carried on with the area now within the Communist bloc. Before the war, it had to import at least 30 per cent of its food in order to keep its population alive. By intensive cultivation of land and technological improvement, especially in the growing of rice, it is now 90 per cent self-sufficient in foodstuffs. Nevertheless, it is still highly dependent upon the non-Communist world for the raw materials to feed its fast-growing industries. It is the second largest customer of the United States, taking 8.3 per cent of our exports in 1961. It is also the strongest political force in Asia opposed to communism.

Japan cannot survive as a great industrial nation unless it can find export markets which will yield the foreign exchange it requires in order to buy the raw materials that maintain its industries. Its competitive position in the export market is very favorable because of the great adaptability and skill of its people, and because of its wage scales which are well below those of Europe.

Many complaints are heard against the growing volume of Japanese imports into the United States. Yet we sell considerably more to Japan than we buy from her. We have never by legislation discriminated against Japanese trade. But the Japanese have entered into voluntary export quota agreements covering certain commodities, mostly in the textile field, which have protected segments of our industry from Japanese competition. Europe, on the other hand, has consistently discriminated against Japan. It has refused to recognize Japan as a full member of GATT with the right to "most favored nation" treatment in connection with her exports. Japan has shown understandable anxiety over the effect on her economy of a trade partnership between members of the Atlantic Community. An agreement between the United States and the EEC which recognizes the "most favored nation" principle would be a very real advantage to Japan and give to her greater access to both the European and the American markets if export quotas did not prevent sales. At the same time, Japan must recognize that when she has a tremendous competitive advantage with the lowest-cost labor in the industrial free world, the situation may require the exercise of voluntary restraints such as she has already agreed to for textiles.

Japan indicated interest in admission to OECD, so as to have an equal voice with the nations of Europe and North America in discussing common economic problems. The European members did not assent, but Japan was invited to sit in on discussions dealing with the coordination of policies and programs for assisting the less developed areas of the world.

The other areas of the world most directly interested in "most favored nation" treatment include European nations now outside the EEC, and the nations of Southern Asia, Central and South America, and Africa. The countries lying in the great underdeveloped sectors of the world embrace more than one-half of its population. In greater or lesser degree, each is seriously concerned what the implications of the development of an Atlantic Community, including the trade partnership to which I have referred, may be with respect to its own economy. Their concerns are fully justified, or rather would be fully justified, were it not for our insistence on "most favored nation" treatment for them. The legislation which we have adopted recognizes the importance of allowing these nations, particularly those lying in the tropical belt, to have the freest possible access to the markets of Europe and the United States for their major exports.

But this is not enough. Because of their less developed economies and the fact that they are in many instances struggling with infant industries of importance to their own development, they deserve very special consideration. A pattern for this special consideration was the acceptance of Greece as an associate member of the EEC. Greece was given the benefits of the progressively reduced internal tariffs within the Common Market and, at the same time, allowed to maintain a different scale with respect to its external tariffs on certain commodities which the Greeks felt had to be protected for a time to permit their continued domestic expansion. One hears that the EEC members are none too happy with the arrangement and are not anxious to enlarge the list of nations which receive similar treatment. But the precedent set may and should become a useful precedent in dealing with many other less developed nations.

While many of our South and Central American friends are deeply concerned by the pattern which is being set by the European Common Market, they are hopeful that U.S. negotiations with it will liberalize trade generally. They, in common with some of the African states, have another worry—the preferred position within the Common Market being given to certain African nations which were formerly French or Belgian colonies. With real ground they fear that special privileges being granted to this selected group of African states will mean a future development in those states of products directly competitive with their own. Negotiations in the coming years will be of the greatest importance in satisfying this huge area of the world, so that the Common Market, or the emergence of an Atlantic Community, may not result in the creation of a rich man's club dedicated to making its members even richer while contributing little to the development of other nations.

It is absolutely essential that we make clear to the less developed areas of the world how valuable to them closer unity among the developed industrial nations of the Atlantic Community can be. They will be hearing, as they have already heard, continuing attacks by the Communist powers on the Common Market and on the countries of the Atlantic Community, just as fifteen years ago they heard Stalin inveighing against the Marshall Plan. While it is often said that we are oversensitive to the opinion of small nations whose influence is negligible, nonetheless no nation, no matter how powerful, can afford to ignore this kind of opinion. This is particularly true when that opinion, unfavorable to the Atlantic Community, is based on discriminatory actions. This is a real danger.

On the other hand, if our negotiations are successfully carried on with the Common Market, and if an Atlantic Community is created, these developments should in fact be of tremendous assistance to other nations. However one may define an Atlantic Community, it should not become an exclusive organization. Political and military factors may, indeed must, draw the Atlantic nations closer together in order to increase their own strength and their own well-being, but not as a means of economic pressure, deliberate or involuntary, on weaker nations. The Atlantic Community must be so constituted that its own increasing trade and prosperity will be reflected in the reciprocal benefits for all the less developed nations of the world, not alone in the field of enlarged assistance, but also in the even more important field of increased trade. I cannot emphasize too strongly how important this consideration must be in the guiding of our own negotiations with the Common Market.

Chapter V

The Need for Closer Ties

In the preceding chapters I have sketched out some of the historical background of increasing unity among the nations of the Atlantic Community. I have also pointed out many of the difficulties which appear to make such a concept extraordinarily difficult to bring to reality. However, I think it is important to stress, in the strongest terms, the ultimate necessity of closer ties, and the means by which they may be achieved.

First, let me emphasize that the period through which we are now passing is a truly revolutionary period, and that any appraisal of our own interests, as well as those of the free world, requires a degree of flexibility of outlook unhampered by some of the shibboleths of the past. Earlier I discussed the necessity of a more closely knit Atlantic Community as essential for the survival of free men. I have also pointed out that in the evolution of this greater unity trade policies, as well as military (particularly nuclear) policies, are of basic importance. If an added reason is needed to bolster arguments for the future development of close trade partnerships through the mechanism of the Common Market and future extended trade agreements, the current openly expressed hostility toward such moves by Mr. Khrushchev is in itself a clear indication that he at least fears such progress as a serious obstacle to the Communist ambition of dividing and conquering the free nations of the West.

Unhappily, the psychology of the Western world concerning the need for action varies in direct ratio to its feeling of crisis in East-West relations. When problems such as those of Berlin, Laos and Viet-Nam take second-page rank in the daily news, we tend to forget that basic antagonisms still exist and become preoccupied with national domestic difficulties. All sense of urgency over the necessity for common action fades into the background. During an introductory speech at the NATO Citizens Convention in Paris in January 1962 I made the following statement:

> Must we wait for some great catastrophe to produce the necessary compression of our sovereignties, the critical mass from which great new political energies should emerge? Our alliance was brought to life by the shock of communist capture of the free government of Czechoslovakia and the Berlin blockade. Our present military posture stems in good part from the shock of Korea. In the backwash of Sputnik, we took measures to make our alliance more effective. Now the obscene wall of Berlin, the outlaw breach of the nuclear testing moratorium, the torpedoing of the disarmament negotiations stare us in the face. How much evidence do we need that this hostile force on the march must be met by a real combination of Atlantic force—military, economic, political—and most important, spiritual? Only in combination can we win "the tug of peace" in this century.

Very frequently an analogy is drawn between the situation of the Western world as it now exists and the situation facing the thirteen American colonies in 1779, which led first to confederacy and then to federation of those separate entities. The analogy is valid to a limited extent. It is valid from the standpoint of the common danger which the individual states faced because of their military and economic weakness resulting from the insistence of each on retaining sovereignty. Without the union which they achieved, they might easily have been recaptured by Great Britain and returned to a colonial status. It is also true that their economies, comparatively primitive as they were, were in a shambles because of the barriers which they had set up among themselves as a result of the high degree of competition and their inability to adopt common policies which would give them united strength. Within a ten-year period they found that confederation was not enough and that federation was essential to their survival.

That period in our history marked a turning point in the development of this continent. The achievement of federation came about as a result of two principal factors— the strong leadership of a few farsighted individuals, and the critical economic and military weakness stemming from the lack of central control. Somewhat the same situation faces the Atlantic world today, although the weaknesses from a military and economic point of view are less apparent and the dangers from an alien power bloc sometimes appear less pressing. Basically, however, the desirability of increasing unity remains the same regardless of the fact that, unlike the thirteen colonies, the nations whose interests would be served by closer union have no common language and have in their past a long history of wars and racial antagonisms.

When I said earlier that the times were revolutionary, I was thinking not alone of the fantastic scientific and material achievements since World War II, but also of the new alignments which have taken place. The development of nuclear arms has forced revolutionary changes in military concepts. Greatly expanded facilities, both of physical travel and of electronic communication, have brought every corner of the globe infinitely closer together. Trade patterns have changed tremendously. Our defeated enemies of seventeen years ago have made remarkable recoveries— recoveries even more spectacular than those of the victorious nations. The colonial era has almost disappeared, and over fifty new nations are struggling with the problems of their newly won independence. The European Common Market is apparently here to stay. All these things have happened in a time span so brief as to make it difficult to appreciate or to evaluate their consequences for the future. But an incontrovertible precept to be kept in mind is that we maintain the flexibility of outlook which I have already stressed.

It is easy to assess the tangible gains which have come from the economic recovery achieved in this short span in history. At the same time, it would be foolhardy to assume that in themselves these gains will be maintained without further concentrated effort on the part of the nations who have been the principal beneficiaries. It is impossible to read daily of the political differences which have arisen among the free nations as a result of the nationalistic concepts of a De Gaulle or an Adenauer in Europe, or of some leaders in Britain, the Commonwealth countries or the United States, without fear that the essential unity of these important countries in the free world may be shattered. The question of the possession and control of nuclear capabilities is a continually disturbing factor. Economic interests often clash, and psychological differences may be the hardest of all to overcome. All of these considerations make it imperative that the statesmen of the Atlantic world undertake a revolutionary effort to pull together in a common harness. No longer is it utopian to feel that this must be done. It is the only logical outcome.

As the real problems are confronted and common interests are made manifest the controversial question of sovereignty should fall into perspective. The words of Sir Winston Churchill in his historic plea for European unity at The Hague in 1948 apply as well to the choice before the Atlantic nations today:

> It is impossible to separate economics and defence from the general political structure. Mutual aid in the economic field and joint military defence must inevitably be accompanied step by step with a parallel policy of closer political unity. It is said with truth that this involves some sacrifice or merger of national sovereignty. But it is also possible and not less agreeable to regard it as the gradual assumption by all the nations concerned of that larger sovereignty which can alone protect their diverse and distinctive customs and characteristics and their national traditions all of which under totalitarian systems, whether Nazi, Fascist, or Communist, would certainly be blotted out for ever.[1]

The Atlantic nations, with as much help as they can get from other nations of the free world, must press forward also in efforts to build the foundations of a peaceful world order, always holding the door open to the Communist countries as well, though without any illusions on that score. This means working through and strengthening the United Nations wherever possible. Above all, it means continuing efforts on behalf of arms control and of the growth of law as the buttress of international order.

During the last ten years many serious attempts have been made to bring the arms race under control. Proposals for arms limitation and various degrees of disarmament have been under constant study, but the discussions of all the various proposals made, which have taken place either under the aegis of the United Nations or in special disarmament conferences, have been held in an atmosphere of un-

[1] Winston Churchill, *The Grand Design*, a speech at the Congress of Europe, May 7, 1948 (London: United Europe Movement, 1948), p. 5.

reality and skepticism. The huge outlays for weaponry, and the manpower taken out of the productive capacity of nations to maintain great military establishments, are a hideous commentary on the actual progress which civilized man should have achieved. Any alleviation of this burden can come only with a new era of confidence and trust among human beings. The present cleavage of the world into two camps competing for power makes this impossible. While this situation exists, a more closely united free world is an imperative. In the long run, the world's only escape will be in the acceptance, in good faith, of a body of law and in acceptable policy mechanisms and institutions to enforce that law. This can only evolve through the passage of time. The time span for its realization, however, can be advanced very materially if the free nations among themselves can reach agreement on the essential elements.

Perhaps one of the most disheartening factors in making any real progress toward this end has been the attitude of the United States with regard to the World Court. We gave our adherence to that body, but qualified it with what is known as the Connally Amendment. This provision gives to the United States the right to decide unilaterally what questions are of a domestic nature and hence cannot be referred to the Court for adjudication. We refused to trust the judgment of the Court itself on this matter although the Court, by virtue of its Charter, cannot consider matters which it itself determines are purely domestic. We insisted on reserving that right to ourselves with the consequence that other nations followed suit and the Court, which might have become an important element in the development of international law, has had only minor cases brought before it.

While I was Secretary of State, both President Eisenhower and I urged the repeal of the Connally Amendment in the strongest possible terms. The Senate Foreign Relations Committee, by a close vote, reported a bill to repeal it, but after an informal canvass of the Senate, never brought it on the floor of that body because it appeared impossible to secure a two-thirds vote for its passage. Today, whenever representatives of the United States attend international meetings and dicuss the desirability of strengthening the legal structure for a better adjudication of disputes among nations, the Connally Amendment is raised to show how little faith we ourselves as a nation have in legal processes. It is a source of continuing embarrassment to us. Even nations with very strong nationalistic sentiments, such as France and India, which had originally adopted amendments to their adherence similar to the Connally Amendment, have now repealed them. We should do the same.

Supporting and building up the United Nations remains an axiom of American foreign policy. Public reaction in this country to the idea of a closely knit Atlantic Community, therefore, hinges in some considerable measure on the degree to which the American people may feel that the development of such a community on a regional basis might injure the effectiveness of the United Nations, since a very strong body of public opinion has been built up over the years in support of that body. In my own view there ought not to be any basic conflict of interest or policy.

An honest appraisal of the role of the United Nations in world affairs would, I am certain, indicate a growing skepticism on the part of the American public as to whether that body can fulfill all the high hopes held out for it in 1945. This skepticism is justified. It is justified because the structure of the United Nations as it was created in 1945 presupposed that the nations then identified as the great nations of the world—the United States, Great Britain, France, the Soviet Union, and China—would continue to live in harmony for the maintenance of peace, and that they collectively would join hands in requiring the smaller nations to observe certain standards of conduct in their international relations. The Charter of the United Nations gave to these five powers special rights, including the veto power in the Security Council, which had the principal responsibility for the maintenance of peace. That concept was shattered early in the game when Russia exercised its power of veto so as to vitiate any constructive efforts of the Security Council; and within five years the China sitting in the Security Council had control only of Taiwan and a few smaller islands, while a separate Communist government controlled the whole mainland of China. These two factors led to a greater and greater reliance upon the General Assembly for effective action.

This second body, in which every nation admitted to membership in the United Nations has an equal vote and no consideration is given to the relative geographic, economic or population differences among them, has changed its character completely in seventeen years. During that period the number of member nations has more than doubled. Blocs within the membership, such as the Afro-Asian group, now on occasion can exercise a controlling vote, or at least can prevent the Assembly from deciding any matter of substance for which a two-thirds majority is required. Although they rarely speak with one voice, the less developed nations of the world can, with the help of the Communist votes that are generally available to them, force through resolutions when they see fit, regardless of the views of the much stronger nations in the Atlantic Community group from whom the principal financing for the United Nations activities comes. As a result, resolutions are adopted by the Assembly which are ignored in some instances by the countries most affected by them.

Three times the United Nations has voted to take specific military action. The first instance was in Korea when, by one of those curious accidents which can play such a large part in the world's history, the Russians were absent from the Security Council, and that Council voted without a veto to oppose the aggression of the North Koreans. As a result the Korean War became a war of North Korea at first, and then Communist China, against the United Nations. As of today, the American military commander in Korea is still acting in the name of the United Nations and the UN flag is carried by both Korean and American troops. The United States, of course, had to carry with the South Koreans the principal load, although smaller contingents from a number of other countries took part in the war. The operation was to all intents and purposes financed entirely by the United States.

The second military intervention came with the Suez crisis of 1956 when the United Nations assembled a small force to oversee the withdrawal of foreign troops from Egyptian territory and then to patrol certain areas where its presence has reduced the likelihood of armed clashes between Israel and neighboring Arab states. This contingent of troops, assigned to United Nations command by various nations having no direct interests in the Israel-Arab dispute, is being paid for by the United Nations; but the Arab members of that body, as well as the states of the Soviet bloc, have refused to pay their share of the expenses.

Similarly, when the United Nations, at the request of the Congolese government, enlisted troops to try to bring order into the chaotic situation in the Congo, many members of the United Nations, again including those of the Soviet bloc, refused to pay any part of their share of the cost of this military effort.

I have cited these cases only to show that effective action involving large financial expenditures by the United Na-

tions is at best a hazardous undertaking, one in fact which
would have been impossible if it had not been for the
staunch backing that the United States has consistently
given to that body. It is interesting to note that whereas in
1960 the General Assembly voted unanimously (70–0) for
military action in the Congo, by July 1962 only nineteen
nations had paid their share of the assessments to carry on
the operation. Over fifty have paid nothing at all. It is
inevitable that this record should create a degree of skepticism as to just how effective a role the United Nations can
play.

In spite of these difficulties I feel that the United Nations
must not be written off. It provides the only forum in
which free discussion of international problems affecting
every area of the world can take place. It is still a safeguard
for the maintenance of the independence of the insecure,
newly created nations which make up so large a part of its
membership. It is still playing an extremely important role
through its specialized agencies in such fields as technical
assistance, public health, child welfare, education, and
care of refugees.

The development of a strong Atlantic Community need
not be in conflict with the United Nations, nor should such
a development be viewed with anxiety by the less developed
nations of the world or by any other nation. In fact, the
development of the Atlantic Community into a closely
knit group basically dedicated to international security
and to the rule of law should strengthen the existing machinery for the maintenance of peace. I think the American
people, whose feeling in favor of the creation of a true
Atlantic Community has been growing, are coming to
recognize that this is so.

Chapter VI

Prospects

Just what is meant by an Atlantic Community? During the last ten years a great number of books and articles have appeared on this subject, presenting a host of different views.[1] It is interesting that with very few exceptions, even among those who most enthusiastically support the idea of an Atlantic Community, no clear definition is given as to what nations are embraced within that Community; nor have its advocates been willing to commit themselves to what they believe is the best form of political organization for such a community. I personally feel that, as of this moment, it is both natural and prudent to avoid a dogmatic approach, both as to the nations which should be included at the outset and as to the form of political institutions which should evolve. The various roads to unity now in existence should be kept open. I therefore make no apologies for a failure to include a specific blueprint in this volume.

Agreement on certain principles is, I believe, now pos-

[1] Two excellent volumes compiled by the Conference on Atlantic Community at Bruges, in collaboration with the College of Europe, Bruges, and the School of Advanced International Studies of the Johns Hopkins University, Bologna (*Atlantic Community: An Introductory Bibliography* [Leiden: Sythoff, 1961]), give a digest of the most important discussions of this subject. They are well worth study by the interested citizen as well as the professional.

sible; and I am convinced that in a comparatively short period of time, specifics may well be possible. A discussion now, therefore, of both principles and possible alternative solutions is desirable. Whether the eventual answers will evolve from the quiet type of leadership shown by Jean Monnet in his highly successful sponsorship of EEC, or through wider discussion with public pressures forcing decisions, it is impossible to foretell.

With regard to the principles which should govern the organization of the Atlantic Community, it seems to me that the following are essential. First, the Community should comprise those nations of Europe and North America which are willing to accept the benefits and responsibilities of close political ties.

Second, those political ties and the instrumentalities for making them effective should be of a minimal character, but should be strong enough to act as a cement in holding together and giving a degree of permanence to the economic and military agreements which may be reached. There must be more than an alliance based on fear of a threat from outside, and more than a series of arrangements on trade and finance made for mutual convenience.

Third, the formation of an Atlantic Community should in no way preclude, but should open the way toward, a closer economic and eventually political association of all the free nations. It should not take on the aspect of an exclusive society of rich industrial nations, but should be so framed as to be of maximum benefit for nations in Asia, Africa, and South and Central America which desire to see a more closely knit international society based on common principles. The nations of Latin America have every reason for close association with the Atlantic Community, or even membership in it, for their heritage is Western and the Organization of American States is based on the same principles as NATO.

Fourth, the Community should present a common front against Communist aggression and, while preserving all those elements of diversity which are an inherent part of a free society, should nevertheless be in substantial agreement in support of such principles as the dignity of the individual man, the role of the government as a servant of the people rather than their master, and the respect for an accepted body of law to control or settle disputes in international matters which might lead to serious tensions or war.

As indicated previously, the proponents of the movement which led to the Treaty of Rome envisaged specific political agreements which would make of the European Community a strong political entity. The preamble of the treaty itself declares the intent "to establish the foundations of an ever closer union among the European peoples." As of this writing, it is not yet clear how many of the nations of Europe will become full adherents to the EEC, nor just how far that Community will advance toward political unity. It has in existence today institutions which are presently directed toward the determination of economic questions but might well be broadened so as to be suitable for dealing with a limited number of political questions. In accordance with the democratic traditions of the West, these institutions parallel the political institutions of most democratic nations in providing for an executive, a legislative and a judicial component. Just how the respective weight of each nation in the Council may be changed by the adherence of new nations is still problematical. The legislative branch, the Assembly, is set up by the selection of legislators by the parliaments of the respective nations, much as senators used to be selected in the United States by state legislatures. The Treaty of Rome, however, envisages that at an unspecified time in the future they may be elected by direct suffrage in the six states acting as a unit. The Assembly, as of now, can ask for and receive reports from the executive, discuss those reports and make such recommendations as it sees fit.

From my talks with political leaders and private citizens who are devoting themselves to the problems of greater unity, I am convinced that the great majority of them feel that Europe must settle its own political integration before discussing with Canada and the United States the specific constitutional character of any greater Atlantic Community. While they all recognize that as members of NATO Canada and the United States, with the latter obviously playing the leading role in that military alliance, are already committed in large measure to assuring the military security of Europe, they nevertheless feel that the political relationship of these two countries of North America to Europe, outside of the military alliance, should not be discussed until the principal European nations have themselves integrated to a point where they can speak to that question with a single voice. The same is true in the economic field, although the trading partnership across the Atlantic will have to be pursued at once, regardless of what the terms of the eventual economic association of North America and Europe may be.

The feelings of the Europeans in this respect are quite understandable. They believe that as a unit they will be in a position to negotiate with the North American countries on a basis of equality, and that in such a manner a much more lasting type of partnership can probably be achieved. It is my belief that the present administration in the United States holds the same view. This view has now come to be termed the "dumbbell" concept—the concept which assumes that an economic or political alliance is stronger if it has been agreed to by partners of comparable weight on each side.

It is my own belief that the integration of Europe and

discussions for the formulation of a true Atlantic Community can proceed along almost parallel lines.

Should the present efforts toward political integration in Europe become stalled, a new appraisal would of course be required. As of the moment, the danger of their stalling lies in the very real differences now existing within the EEC itself. General de Gaulle has made it very clear that he will support only what is called *l'Europe des Patries.* Presumably this means a loose type of confederation in which each nation remains completely sovereign and there is no recognition of the right of any supranational body to make binding determinations by a weighted vote. Although there is some support for this position in Germany and Italy and surely will be in the United Kingdom if that country joins the EEC, it is not in line with Chancellor Adenauer's basic policy and is opposed by the Benelux countries, which believe that a stronger federalism is essential.

Just what the eventual position of France will be in this respect is difficult to predict, but it is interesting to note that in May 1962 five members of De Gaulle's cabinet resigned because of their disagreement with him on this specific issue. In addition, when the French Foreign Minister presented to the National Assembly an outline of France's foreign policy in June 1962, the government then refused to permit a vote of either approbation or censure upon completion of that presentation. Almost one-half of the members of the legislature walked out. That walkout and the subsequent positions taken by the leaders of most of the important political parties have been generally interpreted as representing a widespread legislative disagreement with President de Gaulle on the matter of closer European political unity.

Since Canada is our largest trading partner, her relationship to this whole problem of an Atlantic Community is of very real importance to the United States. The recent elections have thrown but little light on Canadian thinking on this subject. It is my hope, however, that nationalist sentiment in Canada, which in recent years has often found expression in strong currents of anti-U.S. feeling, will not prevent our two countries from reaching substantial agreement with regard to the role which we can best play together in the development of an Atlantic Community.

A similarly difficult point arises with respect to Japan, which must be convinced that the development of an Atlantic Community will not be discriminatory against her legitimate hopes of being included in such trade arrangements as may eventually evolve from negotiations between the members of the Common Market and the United States.

I am quite clear in my own mind that the development of a true Atlantic Community, nebulous as it may appear in some respects at the present moment, must nonetheless come through a process of evolution. As a prerequisite, agreements with regard to the use of nuclear power and the respective roles of the European nations and the United States in the over-all military field must be reached. In addition, the trade partnership with Europe, which is envisioned in the administration's trade policy, must have advanced substantially beyond where it now stands before common political institutional mechanisms can be fruitfully discussed. The long-term objective, however, must be kept constantly in mind. I am convinced that neither military alliances nor trade partnerships can of themselves be enduring without the essential binding cement of political institutions. Yet, I am equally convinced that the former are prerequisites for the formulation of the latter. There are, of course, those who feel that there should be a reversal in this order of priority, and that we should be working so as to assure political unity at once on the theory that the military and economic problems are more likely to fall into place if a federal mechanism is first set up. With these views I disagree.

Timing is of primary importance. There is a degree of urgency with regard to moving ahead which is insufficiently appreciated, particularly in this country. To be sure, the whole concept of a true Atlantic Community could be wrecked by pushing too fast at a time when the integrating processes are still under way within Europe itself, while our trade partnership with that integrated movement is under discussion, and while we are still searching for a solution to the problem of nuclear sharing. But the advantages of speed are obvious.

At the NATO Citizens Convention in Paris, at which I had the honor of being elected Chairman, certain specific recommendations were made. In the Preamble to the Declaration adopted there, which I have cited at the beginning of this book,[2] the statement was made that a true Atlantic Community should be created within the next decade. I feel that this is a realistic and attainable goal. With the many matters hanging in the balance, and with political changes which can always occur in the key nations whose assent to such a community is essential, the working out of any exact timetable is a somewhat futile exercise. At the same time, unless some consensus is reached as to the desirability of early action, the sense of urgency may well be lost and the momentum presently in being may be seriously checked.

With respect to the specific steps to be taken now there can obviously be differences of opinion. I personally favor four lines of action, although I hesitate to say that they alone provide the full answer.[3]

[2] The text of the Declaration is given in Appendix I, pp. 79–90 below.
[3] These proposals were among the recommendations of the NATO Citizens Convention (see Appendix I).

The first recommendation is that the governments of the NATO nations be asked to appoint at the earliest practical moment a special governmental commission charged with the responsibility of drawing up plans for the creation of a true Atlantic Community, suitably organized to meet the challenges of this era. I recognize that proposals for governmental action which such a committee might make could well take some time to work out. That is all the more reason for getting started without delay.

Second, I favor the creation, as an indispensable feature of a true Atlantic Community, of a permanent High Council at the highest political level to concert and plan and in agreed cases to decide policy on matters of concern to the Community as a whole. Pending the establishment of the Council, the North Atlantic Council should be strengthened through the delegation of additional responsibilities. The precise make-up and character of the High Council could be left to negotiation, but the purpose is quite clear. It is to try to create a decision-making body which could resolve a number of knotty and long unsettled problems, especially the military problems revolving around the sharing or usage of nuclear military capabilities as well as the degree of conventional military strength which should be maintained by the NATO partners. In thus confronting at the highest level the great issues which touch their vital interests, the Atlantic nations may find the opportunity to move toward protecting and advancing those interests not by separate national action but through the gradual assumption of "that larger sovereignty" of which Sir Winston Churchill spoke at the Congress of Europe in 1948.

Third, the NATO Parliamentarians' Conference should be given additional functions as a consultative assembly (possibly embracing both NATO and the OECD), without specific additional powers. That body is the creation of the legislatures of the NATO states which send delegations drawn from their own membership to periodic meetings. There they discuss NATO's problems and its future and often make recommendations to the NATO Council or to the member governments. But the Conference is not a part of the formal institutional structure of NATO. Whereas in Europe each successive step in the setting-up of European machinery has been accompanied by some form of European legislative assembly to act as a forum for open discussion of policies and also to exercise a watchdog function, no such body is in existence with respect to NATO or OECD or any other Atlantic Community mechanisms which might be established. This recommendation obviously needs to be spelled out, particularly with respect to additional membership where OECD is concerned. Our own legislators, and most of their European counterparts as well, are today very fully occupied with their domestic duties, and those selected to attend such a parliamentary body might well find difficulty in giving the time to their new responsibilities. However, the practical working-out of the details of this recommendation might well allow our legislators to have alternates from outside their own ranks, and so solve that aspect of the problem.

My fourth recommendation is for the establishment of an Atlantic High Court of Justice, to decide specified legal controversies which may arise under the treaties. This step, of course, would have to await the adoption of specific agreements or treaties since the Court's competence would have to be limited to the resolution of differences arising from the interpretation of those agreements.

All of these recommendations, with the exception of the first, follow more or less the accepted pattern of executive, legislative and judicial components, with the respective roles none too clearly spelled out. The third one, however, is worth some added comment. The role of the proposed

consultative assembly follows the pattern of those already
set up in the European institutions, and while no powers
are presently recommended for that body, nonetheless, it
is important to note the historical development of parliamentary influence and responsibilities, as described by
Woodrow Wilson many years ago in his book on constitutional government in the United States.

Not until after the Revolution of 1688 was parliament
looked upon as modern Englishmen look upon it, as chiefly
interesting because of the laws it could make. Not until
the eighteenth century had passed its middle term did it
come to be what it is now, the maker and unmaker of min-
istries, the maker and unmaker of governments. For at least
four of the six hundred years during which it has been an
instrument of constitutional government it was looked upon
merely as the "grand assize," the great session of the nation,
whose function was criticism and restraint, which came together to see that the terms upon which English life was
understood to rest were being scrupulously respected by the
king and his advisers. The thought grew vague enough at
times; the nation once and again lost consciousness of what
its parliament meant; the parliament itself sometimes forgot
for generations together what its trust and duty was; but
every critical turn in affairs brought the whole impulse and
conception sharply to light again, and the great tradition
was never lost.

We speak now always of "legislatures," of "law-*making*"
assemblies, are very impatient of prolonged debates, and
sneer at parliamentary bodies which cannot get their "business" done. We join with laughing zest in Mr. Carlyle's
bitter gibe at "talking shops," at parliaments which spend
their days in endless discussion rather than in diligent prose-
cution of what they came together to "do." And yet to hold
such an attitude toward representative assemblies is utterly
to forget their history and their first and capital purpose.
They were meant to be talking shops. The name "parlia-

ment" is no accidental indication of their function. They were meant to be grand parleys with those who were conducting the country's business: parleys concerning laws, concerning administrative acts, concerning policies and plans at home and abroad, in order that nothing which contravened the common understanding should be let pass without comment or stricture, in order that measures should be insisted on which the nation needed, and measures resisted which the nation did not need or might take harm from. Their purpose was watchful criticism, talk that should bring to light the whole intention of the government and apprise those who conducted it of the real feeling and desire of the nation; and how well they performed that function many an uneasy monarch has testified, alike by word and act.

It was as far as possible from the original purpose of representative assemblies that they should *conduct* government. Government was of course to be conducted by the immemorial executive agencies to which Englishmen had grown accustomed, and parliaments were to support those agencies and supply them with money, and to assent to such laws as might be necessary to strengthen the government or regulate the affairs of the country, public or private. Their function was common counsel; their standard of action the ancient understandings of a constitutional system,—a system based on understandings, written or implicit in the experience and principles of English life. They were expected to give their assent where those understandings were served, and to withhold it where they were disregarded. They were to voice the conscience of the nation in the presence of government and the exercise of authority.[4]

There is no doubt that an Atlantic Assembly, limited as it might be to talk and to deliberation without impinging on the power of decision resting with the individual nations, would have a vital role to play in giving common

[4] Woodrow Wilson, *Constitutional Government in the United States* (New York: Columbia University Press, 1908), pp. 10–12.

counsel and in voicing the conscience of the Atlantic Community.

Any discussion of the future place of the United States in a developing Atlantic Community must of necessity venture into the highly speculative field of assessing American public opinion. One cannot be sure whether it will act as a drag on governmental moves or as a goad to action. But it is apparent that a remarkable awakening of public interest has been taking place.

Some two years ago little attention had been given in this country to the European Common Market and to its far-reaching implications. It was not until Great Britain applied for entry into EEC that we began to awaken to the fact that the movement toward European integration had moved much faster than we had anticipated. Suddenly a great stir of interest was aroused in civic groups, in colleges and in high schools throughout the United States. The EEC became a leading topic for discussion. The President's recommendation to the Congress with regard to a new foreign trade policy heightened this interest and brought home to the American people that what was happening in Europe had a direct bearing on our own economic and political future. Other actions within the government reflected the same trend. By enacting the law creating the Citizens Committee, which met with similar groups from other NATO countries in Paris in January 1962, the Congress had shown its interest in closer ties across the Atlantic. And the State Department in May 1962 established a separate division under a Deputy Assistant Secretary of State devoted to "Atlantic Affairs."

In the private sector a new organization called The Atlantic Council of the United States, with the three living former Presidents of the United States as its Honorary Chairmen, has undertaken an educational effort on a non-

partisan basis to bring to the American public an appreciation of the character of the changes taking place so rapidly
throughout the Atlantic world. In addition, it is giving
American support to two international groups, both with
headquarters in Paris, which are likewise devoting their
energies to the further development and public understanding of the concept of Atlantic unity. An extraordinarily distinguished group of American citizens, recognized as leaders of public opinion throughout the nation, is
active in these organizations.

The educational effort, however, is by no means limited
to any one set of organizations. Some have been active in
the field for a long time and have made notable contribu-
tions to public knowledge. Of these the best known is
Federal Union, which pleads for immediate action to
draw up and make effective a constitution for a completely
federated Atlantic union.[5] From a practical standpoint I
do not believe it is possible to proceed in that way. I have
felt that an evolutionary process—one, in fact, which is
already under way—could alone bring us eventually to
effective and lasting political commitments.

Whether from the efforts of these various organizations
or from the logic of events, the trend of public opinion in
this country seems more and more favorable, at least in
principle, to closer political ties with Europe. The reaction of the American press to publication of the Declaration issued by the Citizens Convention in Paris, and to the
American group's report on it to Congress, may be taken
as a good indication of that trend. Unfavorable comment
was confined largely to one chain of newspapers. In con-

---

[5] Clarence K. Streit, founder of Federal Union, has been a pioneer in
the cause of Atlantic unity. I have great admiration for the tenacity and
eloquence with which he has pleaded his case for immediate federal union,
although I have not been able to agree with it. The most recent of Mr.
Streit's many books on behalf of Atlantic union is *Freedom Frontier: Atlantic Union Now* (New York: Harper and Row, 1961).

trast, a wide range of papers from all parts of the country showed a remarkable degree of support for the idea of moving forward toward an Atlantic Community.[6]

It is often said that public opinion moves ahead of official opinion in a matter of this kind. Obviously, assessment of opinion can be based only on conjecture until actual votes are counted in legislative halls, but I am greatly heartened by the recent achievement in connection with the new Trade Expansion Act. The tremendous vote which this very advanced piece of legislation received in both branches of Congress was, in effect, a reflection of American public opinion. In the testimony given before the Congress, the voices for greater protection and in opposition to the bill extended over many more pages of recorded testimony than did the voices of those who favored the legislation. From all corners of the country, however, the views of prominent individuals and important segments of the press, radio and television gave to this legislation strong support. The trade bill itself was limited to negotiation with the Common Market and other nations in order to achieve a higher level of trade; but in my view there was no illusion as to what the vote on this measure meant. It was a definite vote in favor of what President Kennedy declared to be an interdependent relationship between the United States and an integrated Western Europe, a partner "strong enough to share with us the responsibilities and initiatives of the free world."[7]

In the evolutionary process which I foresee, the Congress of the United States will inevitably have to play an important and, in fact, a controlling role. In the economic field, the two branches of the Congress alone can give to

[6] Excerpts from editorials appearing in a number of American newspapers are given in Appendix II, pp. 91–98 below.

[7] Message to the Congress "A New Foreign Trade Program" (January 25, 1962), *The Department of State Bulletin*, February 12, 1962, p. 233.

the President the powers to negotiate agreements. In the political field, the President can act only to a limited extent since binding commitments of true importance must be made by our constitutional treaty-making process and not by executive agreements. This means the assent of two-thirds of the Senate to whatever treaty or treaties the President might propose. In turn, this means a very considerable measure of public acceptance, since inevitably individual senators are greatly influenced by public reaction. The Chairman of the Senate Foreign Relations Committee, Senator J. William Fulbright, has already indicated his keen awareness of the problem in an extremely thoughtful article published recently in *Foreign Affairs*.[8]

It is my hope that this small volume may add to a public understanding and appreciation of the need for a true Atlantic Community. It has been written, however, with the full realization that events are moving with such rapidity that many changes in the world situation may require reappraisal of the methods of achieving this end. Concerning the validity of the basic need itself, the need for greater unity, I have no doubt or reservation.

[8] "For a Concert of Free Nations," *Foreign Affairs*, October 1961, pp. 1–18.

Atlantic Convention of NATO Nations Declaration of Paris

We, the citizen delegates to the Atlantic Convention of NATO Nations, meeting in Paris, January 8–20, 1962, are convinced that our survival as free men, and the possibility of progress for all men, demand the creation of a true Atlantic Community within the next decade, and therefore submit this declaration of our convictions:

Preamble

The Atlantic peoples are heir to a magnificent civilisation whose origins include the early achievements of the Near East, the classical beauty of Greece, the juridical sagacity of Rome, the spiritual power of our religious traditions and the humanism of the Renaissance. Its latest flowering, the discoveries of modern science, allow an extraordinary mastery of the forces of nature.

While our history has too many pages of tragedy and error, it has also evolved principles transcending the vicissitudes of history, such as the supremacy of law, respect for individual rights, social justice and the duty of generosity.

Thanks to that civilisation and to the common characteristics with which it stamps the development of the peoples participating in it, the nations of the West do in fact constitute a powerful cultural and moral community.

But the time has now come when the Atlantic countries must close their ranks, if they wish to guarantee their security against the Communist menace and ensure that their unlimited potentialities shall develop to the advantage of all men of good will.

A true Atlantic Community must extend to the political, military, economic, moral and cultural fields. The evolution we contemplate will contribute to the diversity of achievements and aspirations which constitute the cultural splendour and intellectual wealth of our peoples.

The Atlantic Convention, keeping this ideal constantly in view, recommends the following measures which, in its opinion, would foster the necessary cohesion of the West, would bring the final objective closer and should be adopted forthwith by the governments concerned.

Summary of Recommendations

1. To define the principles on which our common civilisation is based and to consult about ways of ensuring respect for these principles.
2. To create, as an indispensable feature of a true Atlantic Community, a permanent High Council at the highest political level, to concert and plan, and in agreed cases to decide policy on matters of concern to the Community as a whole. Pending the establishment of the Council, the Convention recommends that the North Atlantic Council be strengthened through the delegation of additional responsibilities.
3. To develop the NATO Parliamentarians' Conference into a consultative Assembly which would review the work of all Atlantic institutions and make recommendations to them.
4. To establish an Atlantic High Court of Justice, to decide

specified legal controversies which may arise under the Treaties.

5. To harmonize political, military and economic policy on matters affecting the Community as a whole.

6. That the North Atlantic Council treat the development of an agreed NATO policy with respect to nuclear weapons as a matter of urgency.

7. That it welcomes the development, progress and prospective expansion of the European economic institutions, and the spirit of President Kennedy's statement that a trade partnership be formed between the United States and the European Economic Community, the basis of an Atlantic Economic Community, open to other nations of the free world.

8. That the Atlantic nations, acknowledging the right of every people to freedom, independence and pursuit of happiness, cooperate on a larger scale with the developing nations in their economic programmes, through direct and multilateral action; through the acceleration of investments; and especially through measures which would increase both the volume and value of their exports, including special tariff concessions for their exports.

9. That the Atlantic Community take steps to help improve all their economies, so that the proportionate economic and social potential of all will be less unequal.

10. That the Atlantic nations, noting the destruction of the national independence and the human rights of many peoples in Eastern and Central Europe, reaffirms its belief that the problem of these captive nations should be resolved in accordance with the principles of both individual liberty and national self-determination.

11. To create an Atlantic Council for youth, education and culture in order to draw up Atlantic plans for exchanges of young people, students and teachers and for the purposes of scientific and cultural collaboration.

12. That the NATO Governments promptly establish a Special Governmental Commission to draw up plans within two

years for the creation of a true Atlantic Community, suitably organised to meet the political, military and economic challenges of this era.

Resolutions

We, the delegates to the Atlantic Convention of NATO Nations, in meeting assembled, taking note of the recommendations of the NATO parliamentarians' Conference of 17 November, 1961, that an organised Atlantic Community be created, have adopted the following documents:

Part I—Political and Economic Questions

A. Special Governmental Commission to Propose Organisational Changes

Call upon the Governments of the NATO countries to draw up plans within two years for the creation of an Atlantic Community suitably organised to meet the political, military and economic challenges of this era. To this end they should, within the earliest practicable period, appoint members to a Special Governmental Commission on Atlantic unity. The Commission should study the organisation of the Atlantic Community, particularly in the light of the recommendations of this Convention, and it should be instructed to propose such reforms and simplifications of existing institutions, and such new institutions, as may be required.

B. Institutions

1. Recommend, as an indispensable feature of a true Atlantic Community, the creation at the highest political level, of a Permanent High Council, whose competence would extend to political, economic, military and cultural matters. Such

a Council, assisted by a Secretariat, would not only prepare and concert policies on current questions and, in defined cases, decide them by a weighted, qualified majority vote, but would also undertake long-term planning and propose initiatives on matters of concern to the Community. All members of the Community would be represented on the Council.

Whether this High Council be a new institution or a development of the North Atlantic Council should be a matter of recommendation by the Special Governmental Commission. In any event, however, pending the establishment of the Atlantic Community, the members of the Convention urgently request their governments to reinforce and develop the North Atlantic Treaty Organisation as a political centre. To this end, the Convention recommends that the North Atlantic Council be strengthened through the delegation of additional jurisdiction. Where authority for decision is delegated to the North Atlantic Council by governments, it should employ a weighted majority vote.

2. Propose that the NATO Parliamentarians' Conference be developed into a consultative Atlantic Assembly, to meet at stated intervals, or upon the call of its President or otherwise, to receive reports regularly transmitted to it by the Secretaries General of other Atlantic bodies; to raise questions for and to consider, debate and review the work of all Atlantic institutions, and make recommendations to other Atlantic bodies and governments on questions of concern to the Atlantic Community. A permanent secretariat and an annual budget should be provided for the Atlantic Assembly to insure continuity. In certain defined cases, recommendations should be by weighted majority vote. Members of the Atlantic Assembly would be selected by member governments in accordance with their constitutional procedures. They need not necessarily be Parliamentarians. The members thus chosen would have the power to elect a limited number of additional members of equal status.

3. Recommend the creation of a High Court of Justice, reserved to the Atlantic Community, in order to settle legal dif-

ferences between members and between members and the organisations arising from the interpretation and application of treaties.

C. Policies

The institutions of the Atlantic Community should harmonise those policies of its members affecting the interests of the Community as a whole, and contribute to the development of Community methods in planning, considering and executing such policies.

1. A primary objective is the continuing expression through national and international action of an overriding community of national interests in political and military policy. Closer and more effective action in this field should not await the growth of Community institutions (see Paragraph 2, above); the development of an agreed NATO policy with respect to nuclear weapons should, among other immediate problems, be treated as a matter of urgency by the North Atlantic Council.

2. A second cardinal policy objective is to realise the opportunities for economic progress available through the creation and development of the Atlantic Community. The expanding European Economic Community is an economic advantage not only for its members, but for North America and the free world as well. The Convention welcomes the spirit of President Kennedy's recent statement that a trade partnership be formed between the United States and the European Economic Community. We hope that the negotiations envisaged by President Kennedy succeed in establishing a relationship which would constitute the nucleus of an Atlantic Economic Community, within the framework of Community institutions, and open to all other qualified countries. Such a development would be of advantage to all countries, and particularly to those which participate directly in it. Among the fruits of this expanding Community would be its stimulus to competition, investment and more rapid growth in the mass markets appropriate to the modern technological age, with progressive reductions in tariffs and other barriers to trade.

3. Another important goal of the Atlantic nations is to co-operate with those developing nations which wish to do so in their efforts to overcome the burden of poverty, which may well be that of a falling per capita income in some countries. The Convention recommends that the Atlantic Community increase its already considerable participation in development programmes of this kind, through direct financial and technical measures; through increased shares in United Nations programmes, OECD programmes and other multilateral efforts; and above all through policies which favour commerce with and investment in the development countries, such as the abolition of tariffs on tropical and primary products, and the reduction and, under agreed circumstances, even the eventual abolition of tariffs on their other products. The Convention also recommends the development of equitable and agreed programmes for the acceleration of investments, and for the protection of investors against political risks.

4. An important goal of the Atlantic Community's economic policies should be to help raise the standard of living and the level of economic activity of the different segments of the Atlantic Community, so that the proportional economic and social potential of all the members will be relatively less unequal.

5. In view of the hundreds of millions of hungry people alive today, and the prospect that, if the present trends continue, there will be three thousand million more people added to the population in the next generation, the Convention recommends that the Atlantic Community should address itself forthwith to the population problem.

6. Since Soviet expansion has destroyed the effective national independence of many peoples in Eastern and Central Europe, denying to their individual members the free exercise of their religious rights and democratic liberties—with all the attendant injurious effects upon the general climate of European security and progress, the Convention affirms its recognition of the inalienable rights of all nations to assume freely the responsibilities of self-determination and self-government, and ex-

presses its firm belief that the problem of the captive nations of Eastern and Central Europe should be resolved in accordance with the rights and principles of both individual liberty and national self-determination.

7. As most governments of the Atlantic Community countries have accepted the obligatory clause of the Statute of the International Court of Justice at The Hague, the Convention recommends that all members of the Atlantic Community accept this obligatory clause.

Part II—Moral and Cultural Questions

A. The Atlantic Convention of NATO nations

Declares that the basic moral and spiritual principles upon which the lives and acts of the nations forming the Atlantic Community are based are as follows:

1. The purpose of political and economic institutions is the protection and promotion of the rights, liberties and duties which enable every human being to fulfill his or her spiritual vocation;
2. Liberty is inseparable from responsibility, which implies recognition of a moral law to which men, as individuals and in groups, are subject;
3. Liberty is inseparable from the duties of men toward one another, which implies the obligation to ensure that all men gradually attain physical and moral well-being;
4. Liberty is inseparable from tolerance, which recognises the right to free discussion of all opinions which are not in violation of the very principles of civilisation;
5. There can be no freedom without variety, the natural result of the different origins and varying achievements of different peoples in all fields. But this variety should not entail disunity. On the contrary, retaining the common factors, it should become the permanent force impelling the peoples of our Western civilisation to unite;

6. Freedom is inseparable from the spirit of objective truth, which must restore to words the exact meaning they have in the Free World.

And therefore *invites* member countries:

1. To defend and promote the values and principles of civilisation by means of education, publications, lectures, radio, the cinema and television;
2. To uphold in their conduct with all nations the ethics and values of Western civilisation and by their example to impress on others that discord and disunity result when they are not observed;
3. To defend these values and principles against intellectual and moral subversion within the Community;
4. To try to establish an atmosphere of mutual understanding between the members of the Atlantic Community, appreciating to the full the riches of their diversity;
5. To demonstrate to all peoples that respect for these values and principles can alone make a technological civilisation an instrument for improving the physical and moral well-being of mankind.

Reconstruction of the Acropolis: To decide that the Acropolis shall become the symbol of our culture and the shrine of our Alliance and to call upon governments to consider how this resolution might be given concrete form.

B. The Atlantic Convention of NATO nations:

Considering that a major obstacle to the formation of real European and Atlantic Communities is the difference in language and therefore in mentalities and ways of thinking;

Considering that this language barrier is particularly prejudicial to the scientific co-operation upon which the Western potential depends:

Invites the Governments of NATO nations, and such other countries as may be inspired by the same ideal, to convene an Atlantic Council consisting of Ministers of Education, Ministers for Scientific Affairs, cultural and educational authorities and representatives of universities and scientific research organisations, with a view to:

1. Determining the comprehensive aims of an education likely to promote the ideals and purposes of the Atlantic Community, studying ways and means of implementing the principles laid down, and periodically reviewing the results achieved.

2. Organising:
   a bold Atlantic Plan for Youth and Education with the aim of furthering the study of languages and the widest possible exchange of students, teachers and youth leaders and of workers in industry and agriculture,
   a programme of scientific co-operation among the scientists and the scientific institutions of the countries of the Community,
   both of the above being financed by all participating nations.

Within the framework of the above recommendations, the Convention *draws the attention of governments* to the following points:

a. Alongside the study and use of foreign languages, it is essential that mutual understanding be developed between men with different ways of thinking from all parts of the free world, including those of the emergent nations. This programme should in the first place benefit university students, as many as possible of whom should be enabled to spend at least one year of their course in a university or other advanced training establishment where teaching is in a language other than their own.
   However, in the case of the most promising citizens of the emergent nations this programme should have a special priority, since their intellectual hunger must be satisfied at all costs.
   Steps will have to be taken to ensure that such periods spent at foreign universities or other establishments do not preju-

dice the career of the student concerned but rather confer advantages upon him in the form of either a degree valid in his own country or a new type of degree specially created for the purpose of enabling him, for instance, to exercise his profession either in his own country or in that where he has completed one or more years of study, always providing that his knowledge of the two languages is sufficient.

b. It is to be hoped that, in the future, those who have pursued such a course of training, which would subsequently be supplemented by exchanges of civil servants between Atlantic nations, will be given priority in selection for posts as officials required to take part in international negotiations.

c. It should be made possible for teachers, and particularly university teachers, research workers and curators of museums and art galleries, either to be seconded periodically to equivalent foreign organisations, or to establish close contacts with them. Although it may not be immediately possible for all Atlantic Community countries, the introduction of the system of the "sabbatical year" for professors and research workers would be generally desirable.

d. In the field of scientific documentation and co-operation, it would be necessary to supplement existing organs by setting up a Scientific Documentation Centre responsible, among other things, for the translation and distribution of the principal articles, reports and other publications appearing throughout the world, and which have not yet been distributed by other agencies. The Committee considers this a most urgent matter.

e. The "pairing-off" of universities and other advanced educational establishments of different languages within the Community should be encouraged and intensified.

f. The establishment and exchange of comparable statistics on education and research in the Atlantic Community countries should be assured.

C. Recommends that these proposals be studied further by the Atlantic Institute to assist in the accomplishment of these tasks in co-operation with existing agencies, such as the Council for Cultural Co-operation of the Council of Europe to avoid duplication of effort.

General Resolution

The Atlantic Convention of NATO Nations requests its President to forward the foregoing Declaration and Resolutions to the NATO Council and to the NATO Parliamentarians' Conference at the earliest possible date, and that the delegates to this Convention report the same to their respective Governments or Legislative authorities at their earliest convenience.

Appendix II

Editorial Comment in the American Press on the Subject of Atlantic Unity

---

Fall River, Mass., *Herald-News*, Jan. 6, 1962: "The fact that both Herter and Clayton are willing to head the delegation indicates that on the very highest political levels in the country, the idea of an eventual Atlantic union is being taken seriously. The proceedings at the convention in Paris may not seem immediately important, but it would be a good thing for Americans to study them. They may be more important than they seem."

Philadelphia, Pa., *Inquirer*, Jan. 8, 1962: "The most priceless possession of the North Atlantic community is liberty. Let this be the keynote of the convention in Paris. Let the peoples and governments of NATO show the world, by example, that peaceful cooperation within the framework of freedom is both an ideal and a practical relationship—among countries as well as individuals."

Dayton, Ohio, *Journal Herald*, Jan. 9, 1962: ". . . we move toward unity. We build a citadel of freedom on both sides of the Atlantic. We prepare to exert the combined weight of our military, economic, political, psychological and spiritual resources to win the fierce struggle with communism. The Atlantic Convention takes us in the right direction."

Baltimore, Md., *Sun,* Jan. 9, 1962: "Nothing concrete will come out of the convention now opened. It is another talk-fest. At the most, its members can take home some recommendations. But it ought not to be underrated. This meeting is the beginning of a conditioning process that can very well lead to important results."

Boston, Mass., *Herald,* Jan. 10, 1962: "The very fact that the Convention exists is proof that one part of the world community is not waiting for catastrophe to push it into united action. In the Atlantic theater the fifteen postwar years have already witnessed a greater 'compression of sovereignty' than the previous five hundred years. . . . Their course is set 'between inertia and utopia.' The common sense proposals of the convention . . . should be studied with the closest attention by all the NATO governments."

Decatur, Ill., *Decatur Review,* Jan. 10, 1962: "The temper of the times gives strength to the aims of those planners who insist that only in unity can there be strength. Acting on this principle, the Western nations, after due deliberation, may eventually realize that greater collaboration which the Atlantic Convention considers basic to the welfare of the Atlantic Community."

The New York Times, Jan. 11, 1962: "But as again shown in Paris, the idea of Atlantic Union is on the march. It has already produced not only the North Atlantic alliance itself but also such vital institutions as the Organization for Economic Cooperation and Development, the International Monetary Fund, which has just formed a primarily Atlantic $6 billion pool to stabilize currencies, and various unofficial organizations dedicated to like ends. Years of work and study will be required before the goal is reached; but the goal is no longer Utopian and begins to look like a historic inevitability."

Buffalo, N.Y., *Courier-Express,* Jan. 11, 1962: "It is comforting to recall, as we did in our New Year's Day editorial, that in 1787 a convention of private citizens met in our own country and reported back a plan of union adopted within a few years by the 13 sovereign states which had gained their independence in the American Revolution. Will the sovereign states of Western Europe and North America show comparable wisdom in our own time?"

Miami, Fla., *News,* Jan. 12, 1962: "Of course, the isolationists among us will never accept Mr. Herter's premise that even in the common interest we should yield national independence in the slightest degree. These same people object to the United Nations and advocate our withdrawal. It seems to us, though, that Mr. Herter is basically right in his thesis that this is a contest where we must stand together or go down to defeat separately. President Kennedy's request for broad tariff powers is a case in point. Either we learn to cooperate with our anti-Communist partners economically or the Communists will be victors in the cold war."

Lewiston, Me., *Sun,* Jan. 18, 1962: "Eventually, NATO may give way to an Atlantic Union or federation of states with its own executive and legislative branches of government. That will not be an overnight development, but it is one envisioned as the final answer to the full exploitation of mutual interests of the NATO nations."

Auburn, N.Y., *Citizen-Advertiser,* Jan. 20, 1962: "Thus NATO was created as a framework within which its signatories could cooperate in many ways. It was not merely a military alliance, entered into with a view to deterring potential aggression or beating off actual attack. It equally envisaged permanent common action in the political and economic fields. This is what is intended by the proposals of the Declaration of Paris."

The New York Times, Jan. 21, 1962: "The Declaration of Paris is a starting point on which to build the reality of a NATO extended far beyond its present military emphasis to include still closer economic and political collaboration throughout the Atlantic Community. Atlantic Union, though still far off, can no longer be dismissed as an idle dream."

Houston, Tex., *Post,* Jan. 21, 1962: "The Paris conference has five objectives for the NATO nations. Members will seek to harmonize their economic links; aid underdeveloped countries; make economic aid available to member nations; formulate a unified political doctrine in reply to Communism, and forge stronger political links between NATO nations. Here is a basis for federation of the Atlantic nations which clearly echoes some of the essential ideals of the United States Constitution."

Washington, D.C., *Post,* Jan. 22, 1962: "None of the specific recommendations, however, is as significant as the fact of the Convention and the existence of the Declaration. It is no small thing that 100 leading citizens of 15 free nations met under the leadership of a former United States Secretary of State, Christian A. Herter, and declared their faith in the evolution of 'a true Atlantic community,' exercising political, military, economic and moral powers. The event should be an important milestone along the road to free world unity. The ultimate goal can be attained if dedicated men and women continue to face the realities of the nuclear age with open minds and steadfast good will."

Milwaukee, Wis., *Journal,* Jan. 23, 1962: "None of those countries is ready to yield any basic rights of sovereignty. But there are areas where mutual interest dictates political action. That in itself—establishment of a means to political action and rules—would be significant at this state of development. And the convention was wise to set limited goals which, as time and experience bind the community together, can lead later to greater unity."

Cleveland, Ohio, *Plain Dealer,* Jan. 23, 1962: "The value of the Paris conference lies in the proof of interest by groups outside government circles and the convincing case made for developing NATO into a powerful economic and moral force to backstop its military strength. Much remains to be done, but a seed has been planted. With proper cultivation a worthwhile plant can be grown."

Christian Science Monitor, Jan. 24, 1962: "All this is in line with Article II of the North Atlantic Treaty. This provides for development of what otherwise might remain a military alliance into a community of peaceably co-operating free nations. It is to be hoped the Declaration of Paris will put new life into this hope."

Elizabeth City, N.C., *Advance,* Feb. 2, 1962: "The Declaration of Paris, which is the document of the Atlantic Convention of about 100 semi-official delegates recently meeting in Paris, is the first practical proposal for Atlantic unity."

Springfield, Ohio, *Sun,* Feb. 7, 1962: "Economic, military, and political ties between more than a half-billion of the world's most economically advanced people would make the Atlantic community the most powerful combination on earth. It will take time, but that's the direction we're moving in, are being forced to move in, as our response to the challenge of aggressive communism."

New Orleans, La., *Times-Picayune,* June 19, 1962: "The logic behind the trend of current Western development toward formation of larger political units and integration of these into strong alliances makes such a suggestion natural. The mere mention of cessation of national sovereignty is usually enough to provoke popular opposition, but the elastic 10-year (more or less) timetable for implementing the plan shows that it is not intended to be either thrown together in haste or forced onto reluctant member states. . . .

"In the case of the Atlantic Community, the decision on whether even limited political integration must be considered an inevitable development from economic union will be a difficult one to make. The final shape assumed by the Common Market and the concrete changes its presence works in the structure of the West as a whole will be crucial factors, and while they can be hypothesized, they are not yet evident, much less compelling. As things now stand, a supernational Atlantic community organization is only one of many possible means of strengthening the West."

Meadville, Pa., *Tribune,* June 19, 1962: "Coming as it does from the U.S. Citizens Commission on NATO, the case for establishment soon of an operating Atlantic community assumes new significance. The integration of policies and programs beyond the military unity, which now exists, conceivably would call for yielding of some sovereignty, and this recognition by leading American citizens constitutes a step toward building a community structure. . . . A unified political structure linking the United States and Western Europe would appear to be the next logical move."

San Francisco, Cal., *Chronicle,* June 20, 1962: "The proposition for a delegation of sovereignty was accepted by all 92 delegates who met at Paris. It is significant that 20 Americans, chosen on a bipartisan basis would join in support of such a proposition and put their influence behind a recommendation to Congress that a measure of delegated sovereignty should be transferred to an Atlantic community. . . .

"The basic plan is to build the new Atlantic community structure on the NATO base. There are, however, some disadvantages to this that cannot be overlooked. An Atlantic community resting on NATO would exclude some nations that ought to be in it but could not join because its NATO character would conflict with their neutralist commitments."

Carroll, Iowa, *Times-Herald,* June 20, 1962: "Adherence to these recommendations would develop a strong Atlantic community; there is little doubt of that. And there are persuasive arguments in favor of such a political and economic entity. As we move toward that, however, it would be well to bear in mind that other parts of the world must not be neglected."

The New York Times, June 21, 1962: "The political, emotional, and practical difficulties of this plan are self-evident. It involves the progressive unification of a score of free nations on a voluntary basis—a unification in which the United

States can lead but cannot coerce. History is demonstrably moving in this direction."

Providence, R.I., *Evening Bulletin,* June 21, 1962: "It is easy to say, as many are saying, that the Western World is not ready for any such sacrifice of national autonomy that a true Atlantic community must evolve slowly with the growth of the Common Market and the graduate evolution of NATO. But if we are not ready, unfortunately, our opponents are. If we cannot achieve voluntarily the advantage of unity which the Kremlin already commands by compulsion, the free world is not likely to survive the next decade."

Easton, Pa., *Express,* June 23, 1962: "Compelling advice has been given to the U.S. Congress by the Citizens Commission on NATO. . . .

". . . their representations to the various NATO governments boil down to this: We must yield up a substantial degree of national sovereignty in order to create a military, cultural, economic, and political alliance of unprecedented vitality, capable of securing the cause of Western ideals and freedom against aggression or erosion.

"The fear with which the Communist world regards the possibility of such a Western federation has been made evident in many ways by Sino-Soviet and satellite political leadership."

Portland, Ore., *Oregonian,* June 24, 1962: "NATO was formed as a military alliance to restrain the Communist empire from aggression. The proposed Atlantic community would go far beyond the NATO concept in the grouping of economic with military power and the assignment of policy and command functions to a high council. Are the free nations ready for this movement into part-world government? We do not know. But certainly the report merits reasoned debate rather than demagogic speeches in Congress."

Milwaukee, Wis., *Journal,* June 27, 1962: "No tightly knit superstate is going to come into being tomorrow around the

Atlantic basin. The American Congress and President are not going to hand over authority to an international body. Yet it seems inevitable and wholly desirable that there be increased unity and merging of interests in the Atlantic community. Time will tell whether this necessitates the surrender of some degree of sovereignty."

Index

Publications of the

COUNCIL ON FOREIGN RELATIONS

FOREIGN AFFAIRS (quarterly), edited by Hamilton Fish Armstrong.

THE UNITED STATES IN WORLD AFFAIRS (annual). Volumes for 1931, 1932 and 1933, by Walter Lippmann and William O. Scroggs; for 1934–1935, 1936, 1937, 1938, 1939 and 1940, by Whitney H. Shepardson and William O. Scroggs; for 1945–1947, 1947–1948 and 1948–1949, by John C. Campbell; for 1949, 1950, 1951, 1952, 1953 and 1954, by Richard P. Stebbins; for 1955, by Hollis W. Barber; for 1956, 1958, 1959, 1960 and 1961 by Richard P. Stebbins.

DOCUMENTS ON AMERICAN FOREIGN RELATIONS (annual). Volume for 1952 edited by Clarence W. Baier and Richard P. Stebbins; for 1953 and 1954, edited by Peter V. Curl; for 1955, 1956, 1957, 1958 and 1959, edited by Paul E. Zinner; for 1960 and 1961 edited by Richard P. Stebbins.

POLITICAL HANDBOOK OF THE WORLD (annual), edited by Walter H. Mallory.

THE SOVIET UNION, 1922–1962: A Foreign Affairs Reader, edited by Philip E. Mosely.

THE POLITICS OF FOREIGN AID: American Experience in Southeast Asia, by John D. Montgomery.

SPEARHEADS OF DEMOCRACY: Labor in the Developing Countries, by George C. Lodge.

LATIN AMERICA: Diplomacy and Reality, by Adolf A. Berle.

THE ORGANIZATION OF AMERICAN STATES AND THE HEMISPHERE CRISIS, by John C. Dreier.

THE UNITED NATIONS: Structure for Peace, by Ernest A. Gross.

THE LONG POLAR WATCH: Canada and the Defense of North America, by Melvin Conant.

LATIN AMERICA: Diplomacy and Reality, by Adolf A. Berle.

ARMS AND POLITICS IN LATIN AMERICA (Revised Edition), by Edwin Lieuwen.

THE FUTURE OF UNDERDEVELOPED COUNTRIES: Political Implications of Economic Development (Revised Edition), by Eugene Staley.

SPAIN AND DEFENSE OF THE WEST: Ally and Liability, by Arthur P. Whitaker.

SOCIAL CHANGE IN LATIN AMERICA TODAY: Its Implications for United States Policy, by Richard N. Adams, John P. Gillin, Allan R. Holmberg, Oscar Lewis, Richard W. Patch, and Charles W. Wagley.

FOREIGN POLICY: THE NEXT PHASE: The 1960s (Revised Edition), by Thomas K. Finletter.

DEFENSE OF THE MIDDLE EAST: Problems of American Policy (Revised Edition), by John C. Campbell.

COMMUNIST CHINA AND ASIA: Challenge to American Policy, by A. Doak Barnett.

FRANCE, TROUBLED ALLY: De Gaulle's Heritage and Prospects, by Edgar S. Furniss, Jr.

THE SCHUMAN PLAN: A Study in Economic Cooperation, 1950-1959, by William Diebold, Jr.

SOVIET ECONOMIC AID: The New Aid and Trade Policy in Underdeveloped Countries, by Joseph S. Berliner.

RAW MATERIALS: A Study of American Policy, by Percy W. Bidwell.

NATO AND THE FUTURE OF EUROPE, by Ben T. Moore.

AFRICAN ECONOMIC DEVELOPMENT, by William A. Hance.

INDIA AND AMERICA: A Study of Their Relations, by Phillips Talbot and S. L. Poplai.

JAPAN BETWEEN EAST AND WEST, by Hugh Borton, Jerome B. Cohen, William J. Jorden, Donald Keene, Paul F. Langer and C. Martin Wilbur.

NUCLEAR WEAPONS AND FOREIGN POLICY, by Henry A. Kissinger.

MOSCOW-PEKING AXIS: Strengths and Strains, by Howard L. Boorman, Alexander Eckstein, Philip E. Mosely and Benjamin Schwartz.

CLIMATE AND ECONOMIC DEVELOPMENT IN THE TROPICS, by Douglas H. K. Lee.

RUSSIA AND AMERICA: Dangers and Prospects, by Henry L. Roberts.

FOREIGN AFFAIRS BIBLIOGRAPHY, 1942–1952, by Henry L. Roberts.